The Naturalists

Pioneers of Natural History

The Naturalists
Pioneers of Natural History

Alan C Jenkins

Hamish Hamilton
London

Contents

For Nan

A *Webb & Bower* BOOK

Edited, designed and produced by
Webb & Bower Limited, Exeter, England

Designed by Vic Giollitto
Picture Research by Anne-Marie Erlich

© Text: Alan C. Jenkins 1978
© Illustrations and design: Webb & Bower Limited 1978

British Library Cataloguing in Publication Data
Jenkins, Alan Charles
   The naturalists.
   1. Naturalists – History
   I. Title
   500.9'2'2   QH26

ISBN 0-241-89999-0

First published in Great Britain 1978
by Hamish Hamilton Limited
90 Great Russell Street
London WC1B 3PT

Printed in Great Britain by
Jolly & Barber Limited
Rugby, Warwickshire

Bound by Webb, Son & Company
London and Wales

1 The Earliest Pioneers

It could be said that the earliest naturalist was primitive man, who depended entirely on his skill as hunter, fisherman, gatherer. It is true that he came to regard natural phenomena, disasters especially, as having been caused by evil spirits. The overwhelming tide that caused him to flee to higher ground, for instance, was the work of some mysterious and vengeful underwater creature; the fire and all-consuming lava from an erupting volcano had spewed from some fearful dragon's throat; the lightning that sent out its death-dealing strokes was, equally, caused by a malign being lurking in the clouds. Later on of course such spirits were promoted to gods and given names such as Poseidon and Zeus.

Even in hunting Man's superstition reigned. Good hunting was ensured by the portrayal of animals on the walls of caves. Or it could be that such paintings were to accustom the hunter to what he would have to face and help him identify his prey. When he had hunted successfully, the spirit of an animal had to be appeased, for Man was convinced that wild creatures were inhabited by spirits just as he and his fellows were. In every corner of the earth the hunter tried to mollify his victim. The pygmy of Central Africa assured the elephant he had brought down that it was all an unfortunate accident:

> Our spear has gone astray,
> O Father Elephant!
> We did not wish to kill you,
> O Father Elephant!
> It is not the warrior who has taken away
> your life,
> Your hour had come.
> Do not return to trample on our huts,
> O Father Elephant!★

And far away in the north, the Lapps donned their finest raiment when they went hunting the bear. Having killed him, they recited a song in praise of his valour and assured him that it was not they who had killed him. Somebody else had done the deed. In time the Lapps learned to blame such acts of slaughter on the Russians. As an additional precaution, however, their womenfolk disguised them by spitting alder-dye over their faces on their return home, and the prudent hunters crawled into their tents at the rear, lest the bear's ghost was lying in wait for them at the entrance.

★C. M. Bowra, 'O Father Elephant', *Primitive Song* (1968).

The painting and carving of animals (the Stone Age examples here and overleaf are from Norway) had an element of magic, being reminiscent of the primitive – and medieval – practice of making an effigy of an enemy and sticking pins into it in order to bring harm to the actual person. Thrust a spear or an arrow into the image of an animal and you might have better luck in your hunting. Even in modern times an African hunter would plunge his spear into the hoof-print of his quarry in the hope of ensuring its capture.

Leaving aside these primitive insurance policies, the hunter was from necessity of a practical turn of mind. Life was intensely difficult, for, while game abounded on all sides, the hunter's weapons and traps were extremely unsophisticated. Bow and arrow or spear called for far greater skill than the murderous gun of later generations. To succeed, the primitive hunter had to be an expert not only in hurling a spear or rigging up a fall-trap, but in knowing the habits of his intended victim – knowing its weaknesses, its strength and its habitat. He had to be able to track an animal for miles if necessary by its spoor. He had to know why perhaps insignificant creatures were behaving in a certain way – why monkeys were making a fuss or why the jackal was calling in a peculiar fashion. He had to know when the wild geese would return. He

had to discover the favourite feeding-grounds of the elephant so that he could lay his pit-traps in suitable places.

In other words, he had to be a naturalist. His very existence depended on his knowledge of wildlife. And of course he had to be something of a botanist, too. Otherwise what hostile beasts had failed to accomplish with

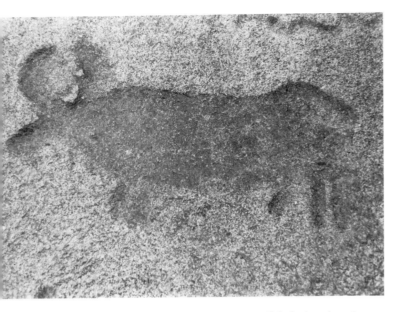

Aristotle's writings are rich in picturesque material. He declared that a lion's bones were so hard that sparks flashed from them if they were struck; that swallows hibernated; that the sex of goat-kids depended on which way the wind was blowing when the buck served the nanny; that the reproduction of certain species could be brought about by spontaneous generation; that the ass detested the lizard because it sometimes got into the manger and prevented the ass from eating by inconsiderately exploring its nostril. He declared that snakes had an insatiable thirst for wine. 'Knowing this, men sometimes hunt them by placing saucers of wine in the walls that snakes frequent. The snakes become drunk on the wine and are thus easily caught.' He described the 'Manticore' as having a triple row of teeth in both jaws, being as big and hairy as a lion but with a face like a man's, as possessing a sting in its tail and having the ability to shoot off spines from it like arrows.

Today, all this seems very quaint. What is extraordinary is that the man who indulged in or repeated such fantasies could at the same time be so perceptive about other aspects of natural history. In contrast with his predeliction for such yarns, Aristotle knew the supreme importance of observation and of accurate, preferably first-hand, information. He studied the migratory movements of birds and fishes. He noted how the hen partridge would lure away fox or man from her young ones by feigning injury. He wrote about the woodpecker's habit of wedging nuts in the bark of trees, the more easily to crack them. He speculated on the importance of territorial rights among animals. He was particularly knowledgeable about marine life in general and fishes in particular:

The special characteristics of the true fishes consist in the branchiae and fins, the majority having four fins, but the elongated ones, such as the eels, having only two. Some, such as the Muraena, lack fins altogether. The Rays swim with the whole of their body, which is spread out. The branchiae are sometimes furnished with an opercle or gill-covering, sometimes without one, as in the case of the cartilaginous fishes.

No fish has hairs or feathers. Most are covered with scales, but some have a rough or smooth skin. The tongue is hard, often bearing teeth; and sometimes so

claws or fangs or tusks, certain wild fruits, berries or mushrooms might achieve, by different but no less unpleasant means.

Moreover, he had a proper respect for nature. He killed only enough to feed and clothe himself. It is said in extenuation of blood sports such as fox-hunting or stag-hunting that the hunting instinct is innate in man. But primitive man never hunted for sport.

As for 'natural history', it was only when Man ceased to be primarily a hunter – or even a nomadic pastoralist – when he settled down to grow crops and eventually build cities, with all their nascent culture, that he began to look upon nature with a 'scientific' eye. 'An intimate knowledge of natural history became less an essential to existence and more an intellectual luxury of the curious.'[*]

The first to indulge in this 'luxury' in any significant way was Aristotle. He was born nearly 2,400 years ago – in 384 B.C. – in Macedonia, where his father was physician to the royal family. It was a helpful connection, for Philip of Macedonia appointed Aristotle as tutor to his son, the future Alexander the Great. However, Aristotle's influence over his pupil does not seem to have been particularly auspicious. After ravaging the Middle East with his all-conquering armies and storming as far as India, Alexander died of a fever in Babylon, brought on by a heavy drinking bout.

[*]L. Harrison Matthews, *British Mammals* (1952).

adherent that it seems to be wanting. The eyes have no lids; nor are any ears or nostrils visible, for what takes the place of nostrils is a blind cavity. Nevertheless, they have the senses of tasting, smelling and hearing. All have blood. All scaly fishes are oviparous, but the cartilaginous fishes are viviparous. All have a heart, liver and gall-bladder; but kidneys and urinary bladder are absent. They vary much in the structure of their intestines, for whilst the mullet has a fleshy stomach, like a bird, others have no stomachic dilatation. Pyloric coeca are close to the stomach and are variable in number; there are even some, like the majority of cartilaginous fishes, which have none whatever. Two bodies are situated along the spine, which have the function of testicles, and open towards the vent, and these are much enlarged in the spawning season. The scales harden with age. Not being provided with lungs, they have no voice, but several can emit grunting sounds. They sleep like other animals.

One of the best-known instances of elephants being used for military purposes was during the Second Punic War. In 218 B.C. Hannibal made his famous march with thirty-seven elephants against Rome, but most of them perished on the way. According to Pliny, 'The first time harnessed elephants were seen in Rome was in the time of Pompey the Great, after he had subdued Africa, for then two of them were put in gears to his triumphant chariot. Coupled as they were, two in one yoke, they were not able to go in at the gates of Rome.'

The medieval monks often spent years devotedly making copies of precious manuscripts. As a writing instrument, the quill became popular in the sixth century A.D. and huge flocks of geese were kept for the purpose. The word 'pen' comes from the Latin *penna*, a feather. This illustration, too, is from Aristotle.

This beautiful example of illuminated writing is from a late thirteenth/early fourteenth-century edition of Aristotle's *Historia animalium* in the Bodleian Library at Oxford.

This extract from the *Historia animalium* is worthwhile not only for its own sake, but as an example of how Aristotle's influence continued for many centuries to come. For his findings on ichthyology remained more or less the sum total of knowledge for very nearly two thousand years; until in fact the seventeenth century, when John Ray opened up a new prospect in the study not only of fishes but of nature in general.

Aristotle, however, saw himself largely as a classifier. He it was who first attempted some sort of classification of animals. He arranged them in two 'great divisions' – animals 'with red blood', meaning vertebrates as they later became known, and those 'without blood', in other words the invertebrates. Furthermore, it could be said that he foresaw some kind of evolutionary theory, for he talked of a hierarchy of life, with Man at the top of the tree.

Perhaps it was this, together with his stated opinion that 'some animals share the properties of man and the quadrupeds, as the ape, the monkey and the baboon', that endeared him so greatly to Charles Darwin who, much as he admired Linnaeus and Cuvier, considered them to be 'mere schoolboys compared with old Aristotle'.

Although Pliny lived nearly four hundred years later, his name is often linked with that of Aristotle. This would perhaps not have pleased him altogether, for Pliny (A.D. 23–79) was a Roman cavalry general and tended to despise anything Greek. His interest in natural history evidently developed fairly late in life, his first work being a military handbook, *The Art of Using the Javelin on Horseback*, based on his service in Germany. When he withdrew from public life – to avoid the displeasure of Nero – he embarked on his mammoth thirty-seven volume *Historia naturalis*.

Whilst Pliny discarded many of Aristotle's taller stories, he substituted even shaggier ones himself, which lingered on for many centuries afterwards. For instance, he wrote of certain countries inhabited by men with dogs' heads; indeed, one country on the coast of Africa was ruled over by a dog, whose subjects obeyed every sign it made by paw, bark or tail. One of his most notorious fantasies was to the effect that certain huge snakes would conceal themselves in rivers where elephants were wont to drink. A snake would launch itself from its watery ambush, seize hold of the elephant's trunk and proceed to bite the unfortunate pachyderm in the ear – presumably in the meantime having let go of the trunk. It would then guzzle every single drop of the elephant's blood, whereupon the elephant, not surprisingly, collapsed on the spot. But retribution was at hand; the bloated serpent was crushed to death by the fall of its dehydrated victim!

Yet all this was written in conjunction with a perfectly accurate description of the work of the mahouts and the general tractability of elephants in the service of Man.

As might be expected of a military man, Pliny was supremely energetic and well organized. He was chiefly an avid collector of information, much of it useless even though entertaining. He boasted that he had read (or had read to him) more than two thousand books, and it was his belief that no book was so bad that some profit might be gained from it. Pliny's prolific writings are sometimes lit by glimpses of poetry that belie the ex-cavalryman. Thus on the singing of the nightingale:

> The sound is uttered with modulations, and now is drawn into a long note with one continuous breath, now varied by managing the breath, now staccato by checking it, or linked together by prolonging it, or carried on by holding it back. Or it is suddenly lowered, and at times sinks to a mere murmur, loud, low, bass, treble, with trills, with long notes, modulated when this seems good – soprano, mezzo, baritone – and briefly all the devices in that tiny throat which human science has created.★

And an echo comes down the ages:

> Thou wast not born for death, immortal Bird!
> No hungry generations tread thee down;
> The voice I hear this passing night was heard
> In ancient days by emperor and clown:

But Pliny could at times be shiveringly prophetic as well as poetic.

> It is true that the Earth brought forth poisons – but who discovered them except Man? Birds of the air and wild beasts are content merely to avoid them and know well enough how to watch out for them. It is true that even animals know how to prepare their weapons to inflict injury, yet which of them, except Man, dips its weapon in poison? As for us, we even poison arrows and we add to the destructive power of iron itself. It is not unusual for us to poison rivers and the very elements of which the world is made; even the air itself, in which all things live, we corrupt till it injures and destroys.

If 'Our echoes roll from soul to soul,/And grow for ever and for ever', they also roll from generation to generation, and that quotation from Pliny surely found an echo in Rachel Carson's *The Silent Spring*.

★*The Natural History of Pliny the Elder*, trans. H. Rackham (1956).

It was only natural that men should be curious about the composition and working of the body. One of the earliest anatomists was the Greek Claudius Galen, born in A.D. 131 in Pergamum, Asia Minor. At one time he was surgeon to the gladiators of Rome, so maybe he did not lack for interesting practice.

2 A Man out of His Time

'Naturalists' for many centuries to come were more obsessed with trying to work out a system of classification than with finding out the truth about the habits of wild animals. As for Pliny, though he endeavoured to expand Aristotle's findings, altogether he did not contribute as much scientific insight to natural history as Alexander's tutor had done. His natural history was always picturesque, as for instance when he tells us that only the ostrich is bigger than the capercaillie, which in old age killed itself by holding its breath. In his attempts at classification, at times he got rather mixed up, as in the case of the elk (moose) which he subdivided into two species, both with quite remarkable characteristics.

One species, he declared, was obliged to walk backwards when browsing on trees in order to avoid being impeded by its upper lip which drooped considerably. As to the second species, Pliny seems to concur with Julius Caesar who, in his history of the Gallic wars, portrayed some of the fabulous animals that haunted the Hercynian forest which covered much of Germany.

> The Elk has no antlers and is entirely lacking in joints in its legs, for which reason it is unable to lie down to sleep. Instead it is obliged to lean against a suitable tree-trunk when it wants to rest. The wily Germanic hunters take advantage of this fact by cutting through the roots of suitable sleeping trees without allowing them to fall. When presently an elk leans against one of these trees, both the tree and the animal crash to the ground and the hunter has only to go up to the helpless quarry and kill it.

The influence of both Aristotle and Pliny continued for many centuries to come, mention of dog-headed men being made by Marco Polo in the thirteenth century. The work of the Greek professor and the Roman general was given a considerable boost by the *Physiologus*, a so-called bestiary compiled in Greek in the first half of the third century A.D., and which was probably the work of Claudius Aelianus, nicknamed the 'honey-tongued'.

This first of all bestiaries was by way of being a best-seller, for it was translated into Latin, Arabic, Armenian, Ethiopian, German, Icelandic, Anglo-Saxon, French and Provençal. It was, as might be expected, a pot-pourri

tato uno fiume.

'A doctor holding a "turtle"' in a page from Pliny's *Historia naturalis*. He reported that turtles or 'tortoises' in the Indian Ocean were so enormous that their shells could be used as cabins on seagoing vessels.

spent much of his travels collecting plants. He also compiled an 'encyclopedia' of animals consisting of twenty-six books. In this, his tactics, like those of other medieval writers, seems to have been to gain a certain verisimilitude by scoffing at some previous legends while putting forward his own pet yarns, such as about those unsavoury worms of the Ganges which had the nasty habit of pulling off the trunks of elephants.

Remarkably, elephants seem to have suffered considerable hardships throughout history – what with malicious serpents biting them in the ears and drinking their blood, and unscrupulous hunters setting booby-traps for them when they leaned against the forest trees!

It has to be said, however, that the occasional layer of first-hand knowledge was added to the palimpsest, as in the case of Albertus Magnus who had some experience of whaling, picked up no doubt during his pedestrian travels along the shores of the Baltic and the North Sea. He also wrote extensively about hunting, and for this he relied greatly on the work of one of the most remarkable men of his own or any age. This was Frederick II (1194–1250), King of Sicily, King of Jerusalem, Emperor of Germany, last of the Hohenstaufens. Not for nothing was he called by his contemporaries 'Stupor mundi' or Wonder of the world. He was a man born out of his time and would have been more at home during the Renaissance than in the thirteenth century. He would have relished the company of Michelangelo and Leonardo da Vinci – indeed, Nietzsche compared him with Leonardo. Luther would have approved his denunciation of ecclesiastical corruption. Charles Waterton centuries later would have applauded his insistence on first-hand knowledge.

Frederick's father was the Emperor Henry VI; while his maternal grandfather was Roger I, Norman King of Sicily. Ironically, when Frederick as a child of four succeeded to the throne of Sicily, the Pope, Innocent III, became his guardian. Sicily, which had only recently been taken in conquest from the Saracens by the Normans, was still partly oriental in character, many courtiers being well-educated Arabs. Consequently, Frederick grew up with an uncomfortably open mind, for, like Kubla Khan, he was prepared to accept the best of all philosophies or doctrines. He obtained a Christian outlook on Islam and a Moslem view of Christianity. The

of fact and fiction, and was subsequently expanded, distorted, versified, even Christianized to serve the Church's purpose. And there was a troubadour's version, entitled, somewhat bizarrely, the *Bestiare d'amour*. The last edition, handwritten, appeared as late as 1724.

The 'here-be-dragons' brand of natural history, leavened by some of Aristotle's more scientific deductions, continued in many guises right through the Middle Ages, including the work of such 'naturalists' as the thirteenth-century Thomas of Cantimpré and Vincent of Beauvais. The Swede Albertus Magnus (1193–1280), later sanctified, though not for his services to science, was chiefly interested in botany and he had the good fortune to work for a time at the University of Padua, whose enlightened authorities had established the first botanical gardens in the world. Furthermore, when Albertus became a Provincial of his Dominican order, he was obliged to travel extensively across northern Europe. This, for reasons of piety, he did mainly on foot, and he

The Roman Empire was constantly active during Pliny's lifetime. Jerusalem was sacked by Vespasian and his son Titus – who is fancifully represented here receiving Pliny's great work. London was established as a Roman settlement and Agricola circumnavigated Britain for the first time.

que facit sup manu. z similia
facit qn sedet sup prticas. aut
sedile. z plures oiuerberatones
z iquietatones erut i falcone
qui coz fuerus erat bn portari
qn stabit sup manu mali por
titozis qm in illo falcone qui
seup male portatus e z iuto

aut sedile facit hoc item li
bentr p eo qr prtica z sedile
firmiora s sibi qm manus
quecuq. Illi qui male por
tatus e z z tn adeo e bn man
suefactus q non e timendu
necp d facie hominis necp de
aliis rebz sup adcis remediu.

For many centuries (including the days of Frederick II, shown here in an illustration from his book) there existed a strict system of priorities in falconry. Only the royal or noble were allowed to keep falcons, grandest of hunting-birds. The merlin was for ladies. Young men were allowed the hobby, a miniature peregrine. The yeoman had to be content with the goshawk, but that was dashing enough.

result was that he came to regard all religions as bogus. No sharper thorn for the papal flesh could have been devised, especially when, only a few years beforehand, the Pope had instigated the brutal crusade against the Albigeois of south-western France who preferred to listen to their own personal god instead of the priests, whom they regarded as corrupt. Moreover, Frederick compounded his iniquities by suggesting the confiscation of all Church property, long before Henry VIII in England carried out his work of plunder.

In one way or another, Frederick fought the Papacy politically and militarily all his life, so it was no wonder that successive popes excommunicated him. Paradoxi-cally it was during the course of one excommunication that he carried out the so-called Sixth Crusade, in 1228 – twelve years after the Pope had requested him to do so. But Frederick only did so at his own convenience – and then he had the audacity to gain possession of Jerusalem without so much as a drop of blood being spilt. In a manner that would be approved in some quarters today, he simply went to Egypt and talked things over with the Sultan. The upshot was a peaceful agreement by which Frederick took over as King of Jerusalem. But because he was still excommunicated, only a secular coronation could be held. Anticipating Napoleon by many centuries, Frederick placed the crown on his own head.

However, fascinating as Stupor mundi's career was, one must resist the temptation to stray still deeper into his political and military adventures. Apart from warfare and diplomacy, mathematics, medicine, philosophy, architecture and astrology were among his many interests. He composed verse in Italian. He caused Arabic numerals and algebra to be introduced into Europe. He commissioned one of his resident teachers, Michael Scot, to translate Aristotle into the more accessible Latin. He founded the University of Naples. He greatly enlarged the medical school at Salerno, for he had a thirst for medical knowledge which sometimes went to bizarre extremes. On one occasion, keen to discover which of two men had better digested his food, one having rested after the meal in question, the other having taken exercise, he cut them up to see how things were going.

But chief of all Frederick's interests was natural history. Perhaps stimulated by the example of Alexander the Great, he established various zoological gardens, where Ethiopian keepers tended leopards and apes and camels. He built a system of lakes for the study of waterbirds such as pelicans, cranes, herons and wild geese. He employed a diver to learn about sea animals and aquatic plants. He built artificial incubating ovens in order to study the embryo's position in the egg and the chick's emergence from the shell. Having learned that ostrich eggs were hatched out by the sun in hot sand, he procured some eggs and tried to hatch them out likewise, in the Italian sun.

In contrast to what so many 'naturalists' had done and continued to do, he was never willing automatically to accept Aristotle's pronouncements and frequently criticized him for repeating old legends. 'In our opinion this superstition arose from ignorance' – apropos ancient tales about the Phoenix. 'This, however, we do not believe' – apropos the belief that the barnacle goose developed from a worm engendered by the rotten timbers of derelict ships, and he even sent special envoys to the far north to check.

Much of Frederick's interest in natural history came about through his passion for falconry – an example of the fact that the hunter *per se* must, at least to a considerable extent, be a naturalist. He despised ordinary hunting with hounds or snares as brutish, a pastime only for the uncouth. The only noble sport was falconry, an art that could be learned only from a teacher. Encouraged by his son Manfred, he set out to write six volumes on ornithology, and his *De arte venande cum avibus* (Concerning

From a printed edition of Pliny's *Historia naturalis*. Some of the birds attendant on the handsome capital letter, Pliny describes thus: 'The ostrich is taller than a man, swifter than a horse. The swan – it isn't true that it sings dolefully just before its death. As for the peacock, it is proud and malicious.'

the Art of Hunting with Birds) is a truly remarkable document, not only because it was probably the earliest of illustrated bird books, many of the illustrations being Frederick's own work. Far from being confined to its ostensible theme of falconry, it ranges over a wide field of ornithological information, unique at the time and for many centuries afterwards. Frederick discoursed expertly about migration, avian anatomy, the feeding habits of different species, the defensive methods of raphis running fight with the popes or the Lombards or his arch-rival Otto of Brunswick, he would have been an even more brilliant star in the medieval firmament of ideas. If for nothing else he should be remembered by naturalists for his admirable precept that you could never arrive at the truth simply from hearsay. 'We have only tried to set forth what our own experience has taught us,' he affirmed.

But it was a long time afterwards before naturalists adopted Frederick's principle. Quite apart from his stature on the political scene, he was a giant among pygmies in the realm of natural history. He was a born scientist, and it took many generations before anyone attained a vestige of his quality. The 'nature' books that appeared from time to time continued to consist largely of the same mixture as before, apart from some practical information about the chase and hawking; for most of them, if not all, were about hunting.

One of the best known of these, produced in the latter part of the fourteenth century, has been variously ascribed to Gaston Phoebus and the Norman nobleman Henri de Ferrières. Its original title was *Le Livre des deduis du roi Modus et de la reine Ratio* (The Hunting Book of King Modus and Queen Ratio, alias King Practice and Queen Theory). It was illustrated, and its illustrations formed the basis of a series of tapestries which, after being rescued from oblivion in the early twentieth century, are now in the Victoria and Albert Museum in London.

One of the best known of hunting books, *The Book of St Albans*, was also the first of its kind to be written in English. It was compiled, perhaps surprisingly, by the Abbess Juliana Berners, and it was *printed* by Wynkyn de Worde at Westminster in 1486. Much of it concerned falconry, but much of it, too, consisted of picturesque cataloguing:

An herde of swannys, an herde of cranys, a nye of fesauntys, a sorde or a sute of malards, a cherme of goldfynches, an unkyndness of ravens, a covy of pertryches, a falle of wodcockes, a murmuracion of stares, a tryppe of haarys, a gagle of geys . . .

It is in no way straining for effect to mention such hunting books. Hunting was still the principal link with natural history.

A Sea of Fishes from Pliny. Born in a seaport on the Black Sea coast, Aristotle mingled frequently with the local fishermen. Pliny, too, had ample opportunity of studying fishes. He knew that eels could progress on dry land.

tors and non-raptors, and the mechanics of flight. He observed that though birds such as pheasants fed and nested on the ground, they prudently took to the trees at night. He showed that the cuckoo was a parasite and made use of other birds' nests. Long before Audubon and Bachman tried to show that vultures hunted by sight rather than scent, he carried out experiments on birds by temporarily sealing their eyes.

Undoubtedly, if Frederick had been less bothered by

3 'The Weather's Struggletime'

One of the fish Pierre Belon described had the form of a monk, lived only three days and was dumb, apart from being able to moan. In contrast his friend Rondelet described a fish that resembled a bishop. Belon also described a fearsome sea-wolf inhabiting English waters. His crayfish was rather more conventional.

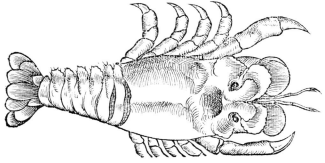

The process of getting away from sedulous and credulous repetition was an exceedingly gradual process. There was after all only one Frederick II. The advent of printing simply meant that the old mixture gushed forth even more profusely. Many ages were to pass before anyone engaged in strenuous and detailed animal watching in the manner of modern naturalists such as an Ernest Neal or a Farley Mowat!

Many of the new books were concerned with mycology, not surprising in an age when mushrooms were very much a part of the human diet, for vegetables like carrots and potatoes had not yet reached the kitchen. 'Fungi ben mussherons,' says the *Grete Herball* of 1526. 'There be two manners of them. One manner is deedly and slayeth them that eateth of them and be called tode stoles; the other doeth not.' In *A Green Forest* of 1567, John Maplet explains that 'the mushroom or toadstole hath two sundrie kinds, for the one may be eaten, the other is not to be eaten'. Likewise his contemporary Master Bullein in *The Booke of Simples* warns feelingly of 'rotten moushrimpes called Fungas', a warning evidently not taken by Henry Lyte who, in his *A Niewe Herball* of 1578, complains of 'being sicke with eating of venimous Toadstooles or Mousherouns'.

In much that was written in such books can be found traces of Pliny, who had not failed to dilate on mycology, including the truffle:

> Amongst the most wonderful of all things is the fact that anything can spring up and live without a root. Now, whether this imperfection of the earth – for it cannot be said to be anything else – grows, or whether it has at once assumed its full globular size, whether it lives or not, are matters which I think cannot be easily understood. In their being liable to become rotten, these things resemble wood.

So much for the 'diamant noir'. As for the boletus:

> Its origin is from mud and the acrid juices of moist earth, or frequently from those of acorn-bearing trees; at first it appears as a kind of tenacious foam, then as a membranous body; afterwards the young boletus appears.

Edward Wotton (*fl.* 1550) was writing, somewhat fantastically, about animals at the same time as Sir Thomas More's *Utopia* was being translated into English and Bartholomew Eustachio was discovering the Eustachean tubes and valve that perpetuate his name.

During the sixteenth century certain doctors were tentatively beginning to question the old automatic acceptance of classical statements. It was perfectly understandable that 'doctors' should be foremost in the growing curiosity about nature, for natural history was a long way from being accepted as a science in its own right and was regarded mainly as a branch of medicine. This was not only because of its obvious herbal aspect, but also because physicians depended on animals for their knowledge of anatomy. The dissection of human beings was deeply frowned upon, though in some cases 'surgeons' had been allowed to experiment on condemned criminals. (And as we have seen, that special case, Frederick II, once had no compunction in gizzarding two of his servitors; on another occasion he gave a condemned criminal a sporting chance by sending him to explore a dangerous rock crevice to obtain an eyas.)

An English name appears here, that of Edward Wotton, whose *De differentiis animalium* was published, oddly enough, in Paris in 1552. He has been described as the first Englishman to make a systematic study of natural history, but he seems to have made little impact. Another doctor, the Frenchman Pierre Belon (1517–64), was one of many examples throughout the ages of the fact that it is not only during this last ultra-democratic generation or two that children of 'humble' families have had a chance to lift themselves out of their background. While Belon came of a poverty-stricken family in Le Mans, his scientific aptitude led to the Church sending him to the University of Paris. His first work, published in 1551, was the illustrated *La Nature et diversité des poissons*, and already in this there were signs of fresh thinking, certainly some glint of gold among the dross. Even more impressive was his *L'Histoire de la nature des oyseaux avec leurs descriptions et naïfs portraits*. This lavishly illustrated book showed extensively the influence of Frederick II, and a sign of the times was the fact that Belon refuted the notion that the bat was a bird. He had seen for himself: he had dissected bats and found that they were undoubtedly mammals.

Belon set a new fashion, too, in travelling far and wide in the interests of science, including journeys to Constantinople and Egypt. Ironically enough, however, he met his death much nearer home, being murdered by footpads in the Bois de Boulogne. We call them muggers nowadays. Another Frenchman, Guillaume Rondelet (1507–66), was also able to travel extensively to the benefit of his scientific researches, not through his own enterprise as in the case of Belon, but because he was attached as physician to the entourage of a nobleman whose patronage he enjoyed, after being encouraged by the Church. Rondelet travelled in Holland and Italy, in whose fish-markets and along whose shores he had many opportunities for marine study. Eventually he returned to his native Montpellier, where he became a professor in the university.

Rondelet's speciality was fish and his main work was *Universe aquatilium historiae*. There, traces of ancient thinking persisted, for he classed not only whales and dolphins but also crocodiles, seals and shellfish among 'whatsoever passeth through the paths of the sea'. None the less, he was less muddled than the Italian Ulysses

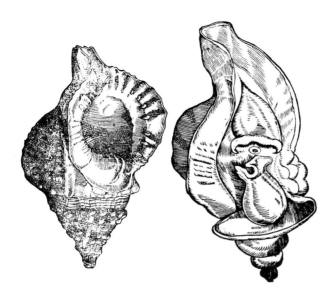

Rondelet in his *Universe aquatilium historiae* (1555), from which this illustration is taken, classed molluscs among the fish. In fact, they are soft-bodied animals usually protected by a hard shell. They have eyes of a sort and a nervous system, but no brain.

Aldrovandi (1522–1605), another medical man – to be exact, a pharmacologist. He laid hands on anything he could dredge up from the past – Aristotle, Pliny, Herodotus, Strabo. In fact, he seems to have been more notable for his adventures than for any new contributions to natural history. These started at the age of twelve when he blithely set off from his home in Bologna on a visit to Rome, without so much as a word to his parents. This inspired him in later years to go on a pilgrimage to Compostella, when he was beaten up by bandits. As if this were not enough, he was later chased by pirates and shipwrecked. However, he did establish a botanical garden in Bologna, where he lectured. Like the majority of 'naturalists' hitherto, he was obsessed with classification. That he had his own original ideas on this can be shown by the title of one of his works: *Of Domestic Fowles That Bathe in the Dust* – which birds he put in a class of their own.

A contemporary was the Englishman William Turner, Dean of Wells. Because of his Protestantism he found it discreet to quit England until Mary Tudor's persecution of the Protestants was safely out of the way. In the meantime he also practised medicine (which of those two words should be placed in inverted commas is difficult to say; perhaps both) in Italy and Germany. All this time he was working on the book for which he became best known, the *New Herbal*, in which he described nearly 250 English flowers. He was undoubtedly the forerunner of many generations of English clergymen who became expert botanizers, right down to the generation of Keble Martin. Turner complained of the complete ignorance then prevailing on the subject: 'I could never learn one Greek neither Latin nor English name, even among the physicians, of any herb or tree – as yet there was no English Herbal but one full of unlearned cacographies and false naming of herbs', apparently a reference to *The Great Herbal* printed by Peter Leveris in

III·CERCOPITHECVS FACIE SENIS FRVCTVM
Cinaræ manu geſtans.

During the Renaissance the technique of woodblock printing made possible the reproduction of illustrations and many picture books appeared. This monkey is from one of Ulysses Aldrovandi's books. Many of his unpublished works still remain in manuscript at Bologna.

Of the herbe be called Ligusticum.

Rosmarinus.

ROsmary hath an hetyng nature / Rosmary healeth þ iaundes/ if þ broth oꝛ water that it is sodde in / be dronken before a man exercise hym self / and after that he hath exercised hym self/ entre into a bath/ and drynke vnwatered wyne after. Men vse to put Rosmari in medicines þ dryue werishnnes away/ and into the oyntment call e Gleucinum. The Arabianes as Serapio witnesseth / gyue these properties vnto Rosmari. Rosmari is hote & drye in the thyrde degre /it is good foꝛ the colde reum that falleth from þ brayn/ it heateth and maketh fyne oꝛ subtil. It dryueth wynde away/& stirreth a man to make water / and bryngeth down weomens floures/ it openeth the stoppynges of þ liuer of the milt and the bowelles. Tragus the Germany wryteth that Rosmary is a spice in the kitchines of Germany/ and not without a cause. The wyne (sayeth he) of Rosmari/ taken of a woman/ if she will fast iij. oꝛ iiij. houres after/is good foꝛ the payn in the mother/ and agaynst the white floures if they come of any inwarde imposteme. It openeth the lung vines/ and it is

A page from William Turner's *New Herbal* (1551). Turner was an ardent reformer and friend of Bishops Latimer and Ridley, who were burnt at the stake in the reign of Queen Mary. His martyrdom in the cause of Protestantism amounted simply to his having his books prohibited and destroyed.

London in 1516. The dean's work was certainly far more serious than that of John Gerard, whose *Herball* (1597) was in any case almost entirely the work of Rembert Dodoens.

Having trained as a doctor, Konrad Gesner (1516–65) was, it goes without saying, interested primarily in botany. Like Turner, he suffered because of his Protestantism, for his native Switzerland was torn by the religious wars and his father, a supporter of Ulrich Zwingli, had been killed at the Battle of Kappel. But, thanks again to far-sighted patrons, the orphaned Gesner came through all the vicissitudes of the time to study and teach and mingle with his fellow 'scientists' such as Aldrovandi. Gesner's first work was his extensive *Historia plantarum*, which he illustrated with some fifteen hundred drawings. The manuscript of this book was lost after his death and was not retrieved until nearly two hundred years later, when it was printed for the first time (1751).

Gesner became increasingly interested in animals and he planned a six-volume *Historia animalium*. Need it be said, he was greatly taxed by the problem of classification, for which he could find little real guidance in the past. Pliny, for instance, had opened his book on four-footed animals with the elephant, simply because it was the biggest; similarly, on account of its size, the ostrich had pride of place in the volume on birds. 'Small is beautiful' had to wait for Robert Hooke and his *Micrographia* of 1665, and for the improved microscope of his contemporary, Antony van Leeuwenhoek. Gesner decided to follow an alphabetical arrangement, though he did at least plan to divide up his work into four-footed animals, or mammals as they were later classed – four-footed animals that laid eggs – in other words reptiles and amphibians (birds, fishes, insects), and lastly the nebulously termed 'serpents'.

The original Latin version of Gesner's work (or part of it) formed the basis for Edward Topsell's *Historie of Four-*

John Gerard had a garden in what is now Fetter Lane. It contained more than one thousand herbs and in 1596 he published a twenty-four page catalogue of them, the first horticultural catalogue on record.

21

footed Beasts, the first illustrated natural history published in English. Topsell, a clergyman, vicar successively of various parishes in Sussex, Hampshire and Northamptonshire in the early seventeenth century, was a man of many parts in a literary sense. His writings ranged from *The Reward of Religion, Delivered in Sundry Lectures upon the Book of Ruth*, to *The Householder, or Perfect Man*. But his great interest was nature and he was at work on his own 'The Fowles of Heaven' (never published) when he came across Gesner.

Gesner–Topsell is very much the mixture as before, with fact and fiction intertwined. For instance:

> A Bear is much subject to blindness of the eyes and for that cause they desire the Hives of Bees, not only for the Hony, but by the Stinging of the Bees their eyes are cured. . . . And when it is time these same Bears betake themselves to their dens for the winter where they grow very fat though without eating food simply by sucking their forefeet.

Yet they could mention, with complete veracity, heavily embroidered though it was, the phenomenon of elephants 'burying' their dead companions with branches. This does occur and the present writer has direct experience of an elephant, which in panic had killed a woman in the Indian jungle, similarly concealing its victim with boughs and leaves as if in contrition.

Yet it is astonishing how long the fantastic side of 'natural history' persisted. As late as 1764, *The Sportsman's Dictionary* repeated one of Gesner's shaggier stories about the elk. It claimed that this animal stored water in a large skin bag under its chin. When the elk was being pursued, the water heated up and it defended itself by squirting scalding liquid at the hunters and hounds, who were severely burned.

Now, the Lapps have an expression, 'The Weather's Struggletime'. This sums up the supremely difficult, varied, fickle, hazardous climatic conditions that obtain in early springtime when they are engaged in the migration to the fells. One day it will freeze enough to provide a good snow crust for the reindeer to travel on. Next, indeed within hours, a catastrophic thaw will set in, making travel impossible, sometimes with disastrous consequences for the pregnant cows. The wind changes,

Topsell's 'Bison', a fearsome creature, 'being maned about the necke and backe like a Lyon and haire hanging downe under his chin, his hornes great and sharpe and with them throgh the admirable strength of his neck can he tosse into the ayre a horse and horseman both togither'.

and a blizzard tears down the tents of the herdsmen during the night. The wind veers again, perhaps tied in knots by the proverbial Lapland wizard, and the weather sets fair and off the herd shambles once more.

It was all rather like this as far as natural history was concerned: an occasional glimpse of brighter thought, then reversion to nonsense, followed by another favourable change of outlook. Within two years of Topsell's death in 1625 there was born a man whose work was to be called variously 'the basis of all modern zoology', 'the foundation of scientific ornithology' and 'the opening up of ichthyology'.

Two quotations sum up the astonishing gap. Topsell, imitating Gesner, could speculate whether

> . . . there be any such serpent as this so-called Hyaena or not, for it is not very like that there is any such, and that this Hyaena is the same self which is described to be a four-footed Beast, for that which is said of that is likewise attributed to this: namely, that it changeth sex, being one year a male, another year a female, and

Topsell considered the whale a monstrous fish. But he wrote accurately about the orca or killer whale, 'which bee deadly enemies to the foresaid Whales, seeking them out, and if they meet either with the young ones, or the dammes, they all to cut and hacke them with their trenchant teeth'.

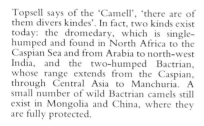

Topsell says of the 'Camell', 'there are of them divers kindes'. In fact, two kinds exist today: the dromedary, which is single-humped and found in North Africa to the Caspian Sea and from Arabia to north-west India, and the two-humped Bactrian, whose range extends from the Caspian, through Central Asia to Manchuria. A small number of wild Bactrian camels still exist in Mongolia and China, where they are fully protected.

that the couples which seem to be married together do by continual entercourse, bring forth their young ones so that the male this year is the female next year, and the female this year is the male next year. And this is all that is said of this Serpent.

In contrast to that farrago is this extract from John Ray:

I saw a wasp, one of the largest of this tribe – I do not now recollect the species – dragging a green caterpillar three times larger than itself. Before my very eyes it carried it almost the full length of a measuring rod, that is some fifteen and a half feet; and then deposited it at the mouth of a burrow which it had previously dug for itself. Then it removed a ball of earth with which it had sealed up the entrance; went down itself into the hole; after a brief stay there, came up again; and seizing the caterpillar which it had left near the opening carried it down with it into the burrow. Soon, leaving it behind there, it returned alone; gathered pellets of earth and rolled them one by one into the burrow; and

at intervals scratching with its forefeet, as rabbits and dogs do, flung dust backwards into the hole. It kept repeating the same operation with dust and pellets alternately until the burrow was completely covered up; sometimes it descended in order, as it seemed to me, to press down and solidify the soil; once again it flew to a fir tree nearby perhaps to look for resin to stick the soil together and consolidate the work. When the opening was filled and levelled with the surface of the ground so that the approach to it was no longer visible, it picked up two pine needles lying near and laid them by the burrow's mouth, to mark, as is probable, the exact spot. Who could not wonder in amazement at this? Who could ascribe work of this kind to a mere machine?

Even though Ray was wrong about the wasp marking the spot with pine needles, that vignette of first-hand observation comes as a refreshing draught after a diet of pure fantasy and is worthy of an entomologist such as Fabre two hundred years or more later.

4 'The Treasures of Nature Are Inexhaustible'

John Ray (1627–1705) was the son of a blacksmith in the Essex village of Black Notley. His interests in nature were universal and ranged from flowers to fossils. Although he was of lowly origin, clearly both his parents were of a 'superior' kind, as it used to be termed, and his mother especially had a deep influence on his subsequent career. Botany, Ray's first enthusiasm, was then almost non-existent as a serious study, in spite of William Turner's efforts. During Ray's lifetime one of the few expert English botanists was Thomas Johnson, whose worthy *Mercurius botanicus* was published in 1634. But Johnson's potentially illustrious career was cut short in the English Civil War. He was an ardent Royalist, became a lieutenant-colonel and was killed during the heroic defence of Basing House in Hampshire against the Parliamentarians.

Ray was not only helped by his mother to fill the gap in knowledge; she also encouraged him in his keenness to make good the lack of information that Turner had bemoaned. She was a 'professional' herbalist in days when the use of herbs for medicinal purposes was not only essential, but in some cases more effective than certain prescribed drugs in use later. The true country herbalist required a skill which was akin to a knowledge of botany. Never mind that these herbalists were as unlettered as the farrier, who could act as a horse-doctor, they had more genuine skill than some of the long-winded writers who got themselves into print, notably Nicholas Culpeper with his absurd mixture of flowers and astrology and alchemy. (Ray himself commented on 'the foolishness of the Chymists who chatter and boast so loudly of the signatures of plants'.)

If Ray was fortunate in his parentage, he was equally so in his village priests, notably the Reverend Joseph Plume. For in spite of being calumniated by the reigning Puritans as a 'tavern-haunter and divers times drunk and a swearer by great and bloody oaths', the parson greatly encouraged Ray, recognizing his latent talent, and got him placed at Braintree Grammar School. It was here that Ray acquired his superb, stylish proficiency in Latin, essential for a scientist. Here too another clergyman, Samuel Collins, Vicar of Braintree, made a vital contribution to Ray's progress. For he was instrumental in getting the sixteen-year-old youth accepted at Cambridge University, first at Catharine Hall, later at Trinity

John Ray realized it was absurd to believe that the universe had been created for Man alone. The stars, for instance, were not made just to twinkle at us. Many were only 'discoverable by a Telescope, and it is likely perfecter Telescopes than we yet have may bring to light many more; and who knows how many lie out of the ken of the best Telescope that can possibly be made?' Jodrell Bank is only one of the steps forward in the path that men like Ray perceived ahead.

College. At Trinity in due course Ray became a Fellow and was also presently ordained, adding yet another name to the long list of clergymen who have been so active in natural history through the centuries.

These were stormy times for England in general, for the 'Great Rebellion' was in progress. For the time being Ray was able to ignore the strife and concentrate on his first work, the so-called *Cambridge Catalogue*, the result of his botanizing in the surrounding fenland, many of whose plants he cultivated in his 'little garden' at Trinity. His interest in natural history as a whole was expanding and he and his friends used to dissect birds and animals in their lodgings – for then there were no such facilities as laboratories. 'I remember some years ago at Mr Nid's chamber I was present at the dissection of four birds. The names of three of them were a Bittern, a Curlew and a Yarwelp; the fourth was like a duck, whose [car]cases hung up in the cupboard over Mr Nid's portal.' Subsequently, horses, cows, pigs, dogs, cats, rabbits, frogs, fishes and vipers figured in these earnest dissections. For William Harvey's discovery of the circulation of blood had inspired the curiosity of the naturalists about the workings of animal bodies.

But though for the time being John Ray was able to pursue the even tenor of his researches, Cambridge itself suffered considerably. To begin with, many of the colleges had been forced to sell their plate in order to satisfy the demands of Charles I in his bid to defend his throne. Subsequently, however, the Parliamentarians had gained possession and Cromwell had many bridges over the River Cam pulled down as part of his fortification plans. In addition, many fellows and students were expelled from the university because of their refusal to take part in the Puritan Solemn League and Covenant. Dissidents are no modern invention.

However, after the Restoration in 1660 John Ray found himself on the opposite side of the fence. His conscience would not allow him to subscribe to the Act of Uniformity. Not only was he expelled from his fellowship, but he was now debarred from practising as a clergyman. What Church and university lost, science was to gain. Nevertheless, Ray, without a parish and even forbidden to teach, would have been in desperate straits had it not been for Francis Willughby, his pupil, friend, collaborator and patron. It was an interesting

With the death of Francis Willughby (pictured here), John Ray lost not only a friend and collaborator but a generous patron. Later, Samuel Pepys, then President of the Royal Society, paid for the cost of sixty plates for Ray's treatise on fish.

partnership, that of the village blacksmith's son and the aristocrat. Willughby's father was Sir Francis Willughby, with estates in Warwickshire and Nottinghamshire; his mother was the daughter of the Earl of Londonderry.

Nowadays various bodies – Carnegie, Gulbenkian, the Arts Council of Great Britain and so on – dispense largesse; in former times the aristocracy and the Church largely fulfilled this function, from William, Count of Poitiers, to Prince Esterhazy. If today patronage has become a dirty word, in the past the arts and science owed many a debt to enlightened patrons.

Francis Willughby was very much a case in point. In gratitude, Ray linked Willughby's name with his own as co-author of several of his works, even when this was not strictly necessary. But whether or not Willughby contributed as much as has often been claimed, there is no doubt that he inspired Ray by his grand idea of a *Systema naturae*.

lib.3 sect.1 Beta VII fo
syl. maritima.

Beta marina.
Hor: pad:

22

Gramen Plumosum Elegans
lib.1 sect.2 Juncus capitulo lanu-
ginoso, Bauhino L. iii. 8. cap lan.
sive schoenolagurus.

Ray's *Historia plantarum generalis* contained nearly three thousand folio pages and was an attempt to cover the botany of the world, a highly ambitious project even for those days when much of the world was still unknown. Ray anticipated Marcello Malpighi (1628–94), his Italian contemporary, in distinguishing between monocotyledonous and dicotyledonous (single and double seeds) in plants.

Materially, he gave unstinting help to Ray, paid the expenses of all their many 'nature' tours, which Ray could never have enjoyed otherwise, gave Ray a home, appointed him tutor to his children, and in his will left him an annuity. And by his unswerving enthusiasm he constantly urged Ray on. For Ray was the essence of modesty, and it was fortunate for him, and for science, that the two men came together in the fullness of Willughby's life. For Francis Willughby died in 1672 at the age of thirty-six, 'best of all patrons'.

In preparation for the ambitious work they planned, no less than a 'History of the Natural World' – to include botany, ornithology, entomology, ichthyology, geology – the two friends set out on a series of journeys at home and abroad. They studied razorbills and puffins on the Isle of Man, went in search of saxifrage and stonecrop on Snowdon, examined fossils in Yorkshire, botanized in Scotland – and even took time off to watch a hurling-match in Devon. In these days of jet travel and fast motorways, it needs a jerk of the imagination to appreciate the effort and discomforts entailed even on such domestic journeys in an age when pack-horses were the chief means of freight transport, when roads were chaotic tracks deep in mud and infested with highwaymen, and a coach journey from London to Salisbury, Wiltshire, took two days, and it needed four days to reach Yorkshire – distances of eighty and 160 miles respectively.

Even more enterprising and arduous were the continental journeys of Ray and Willughby. In a feverish quest for information and material, they visited the Low Countries, travelled up the Rhine, went to Vienna (noticing the famous Hapsburg lip), boated along the Danube, went by coach to Venice. They studied anatomy at Padua, and climbed Mount Etna as far as the snow-line in search of plants. At Rome Ray frequently visited the markets simply to study birds and fishes brought for sale – an indication of the contemporary lack of facilities. He went off to Montpellier expressly to witness the dissection of an ox's head but had to leave France when Louis XIV expelled all Englishmen there. They visited museums, such as existed, examined ancient documents and manuscripts, and bought books and plates wherever they went. It was all by way of being a grand detective chase in search of clues that would help them to present their case.

In a century when, literally, tens of thousands of alleged witches were burnt to death or hanged, when even the astronomer Johannes Kepler 'was convinced that the planets, by their revolutions, produced "a music of the spheres", which was audible only to the sun, which he believed to be the body of a divine spirit; while the great Newton himself accounted for the tangential velocities of the planets, which prevent them from falling with the sun, by supposing that, initially, they had been hurled by the hand of God'[*] – in an age such as this, John Ray saw it as his sacred duty to dispel the dark clouds of superstition and credulity, to lay bare the wonderful secrets of nature.

First, description and classification: they must come before interpretation and speculation. Men must know what things were and how they worked before they could begin to experiment properly. 'When men do not know the names and properties of natural objects, and are ready to believe any fanciful superstitions about them, they cannot even see and record accurately.'

Ray's heart was already aflame, otherwise the early death of Willughby would have cast him down far more than it did. It certainly caused him difficulties enough, for Emma, Willughby's widow, had never liked the dull Mr Ray who absorbed so much of her husband's attention, and had no sympathy for their worthy project. She did, however, pay for the plates in Willughby's chief memorial, the *Ornithology*, which the Royal Society (whose president was at one time Samuel Pepys) took it upon itself to print. But soon afterwards Emma married again and Ray was thrown out of Middleton Hall, his refuge in Warwickshire. He was forced to return to Black Notley, to the cottage he had built for his mother. But at least he had Willughby's annuity and at the age of forty-six – late in life for those days – plunged into matrimony. He married Margaret Oakeley, a girl twenty-five years younger than himself, and they had four daughters, including twins. There is a sad glimpse of him in the year before his death, constantly racked by illness, unable even to go out into the surrounding fields and sending out his willing daughters to fetch specimens for him.

Ray had truly opened the book of nature. His range was indeed encyclopedic. From comparative anatomy he had gone on to examine the structure and function of the living organism. For the first time he had looked into physiology and animal behaviour. Nothing escaped him: the working of the eye, the nature of atoms, the influence of the moon upon the tides, the movement of sap in trees (which John Evelyn refers to in his *Sylva*), the formation of bees' cells, the development of the foetus in the womb, the formation of rocks, the significance of fossils. He was indeed a universal naturalist, and his books were many and varied, from his *History of Plants* to the *History of Insects*. His credo is best summed up by his paean of praise to nature, *The Wisdom of God*, in which he says:

[*]John Aubrey, *Brief Lives*, ed. Oliver Lawson Dick (1949).   27

Two versions of Sir Francis Willughby's home, Middleton Hall in Warwickshire – a contemporary drawing and a photograph taken in 1949. Dr Johnson defined a patron as 'commonly a wretch who supports with insolence, and is paid with flattery'. But Willughby was in a far different category. So was his wife in a contrary way – she did not like Ray.

(Opposite left) By 1950 the magnificent eagle-owl (whose Latin name *Bubo bubo* almost echoes its cry) had disappeared from Sweden, its chief haunt. But thanks to devoted work by the Norfolk Wildlife Park under its director Philip Wayre, successful attempts were made to rehabilitate this spectacular bird which is capable of striking down hare or capercaillie, or even roe-deer.

(Opposite right) The long-eared owl (*Asio otus*) very often takes over an old nest built by a jay or magpie or ring-dove. It has even been known to make use of a squirrel's drey. The scops owl is the smallest to appear in Britain, appreciably smaller even than the little owl but also easily distinguishable by its ear-tufts.

The treasures of Nature are inexhaustible. I know that a new study at first seems very vast, intricate and difficult: but after a little resolution and progress, after a man becomes a little acquainted, as I may so say, with it, his understanding is wonderfully cleared up and enlarged, the difficulties vanish, and the thing grows easy and familiar. Some reproach methinks it is to learned men that there should be so many animals still in the world whose outward shape is not yet taken notice of or described, much less their way of generation, food, manners, uses, observed. If man ought to reflect upon his Creator the glory of all his works, then ought he to take notice of them all and not to think anything unworthy of his cognizance.

John Ray has always tended to be overshadowed by Linnaeus, who never properly acknowledged his debt to the 'English Aristotle', and justice was not adequately done to Ray until Canon Raven's time.★ But the 'excellent Mr Ray', as Gilbert White called him, would not have minded. He knew that knowledge and science were of far greater import than the fame of any individual.

★C. E. Raven, *John Ray, Naturalist: His Life and Works* (1942).

5 Modern Adam

... And out of the ground the Lord God formed every beast of the field, and every fowl of the air; and brought them unto Adam to see what he would call them: and whatsoever Adam called every living creature, that was the name thereof. And Adam gave names to all cattle, and to the fowl of the air, and every beast of the field. ...

Carolus Linnaeus (Carl von Linné, 1707–78) has been dubbed the Modern Adam, though unlike Adam he had many spiritual ancestors and trod in the path many others had attempted to follow. But he did indeed name not only the beasts of the field and the fowls of the air, but the flowers and the trees and the shrubs as well. In his own words, he wanted to name everything from buffaloes to buttercups. And the quotation above is doubly appropriate, for Linnaeus (like Philip Gosse a hundred years later) believed that all natural species were as they had always been since the Creation. He declared that there are just as many species as there were when 'God said, Let the earth bring forth the living creature after his kind'. 'There is no such thing as a new species,' declared Linnaeus, and the title-page of his great *Systema naturae*, the tenth and definitive edition of which was published in 1758, bears this 'dedication':

> O Jehovah
> How ample are Thy works!
> How wisely Thou hast fashioned them!
> How full the earth is of Thy possessions!

And the task this self-confident Swede set himself was to make an inventory of those divine possessions. Now, taxonomy, in spite of its confusing name, which makes it sound like something to do with income tax or suburban transport, is one of the most important branches of natural history. For until scientific classification was developed and formalized, naturalists could not be certain of understanding what their fellows were talking about, however lengthy and detailed might be their descriptive methods. You might get away with describing a giraffe or an elephant, but it would be far more difficult trying to pinpoint a particular flower or bird or rodent.

And of course, to be of universal application, a system had to be in a universal language. That for many cen-

Linnaeus liked to sport a Lapland costume after his famous journey. But the head-gear he is wearing here belongs to a vanished style. Those Lapps who still wear costume either favour the so-called cap-of-the-four-winds or the old conical style decorated with an enormous pompon, visible far away on the fells.

Linnaeus's birthplace. From his humble background he graduated to being honoured by the Swedish royal family, even to the extent of playing hide-and-seek with Queen Lovisa Ulrika. She also collected butterflies.

turies was Latin, and it is astonishing that this should be written off as a 'dead' language. It is still in use today in scientific contexts, and often in the past it was the only common language men of culture could turn to for mutual understanding. Such was the case with Linnaeus when in 1736 he visited London and met such eminences as Sir Hans Sloane, President of the Royal Society, whose magnificent collection was to form the nucleus of the British Museum, to whom he had to speak in Latin, having no English. This was perfectly acceptable in such company as the Society of Apothecaries, whom he addressed, and nobody echoed Jack Cade: 'Away with him, away with him! he speaks Latin!'

Unlike Pallas Athene, who sprang fully armed from the ear of Zeus, nothing in science – or in any other sphere of human endeavour – arrives completely and utterly new. (Even in John Ray's time belief was ceasing in the idea of spontaneous generation such as maggots in cheese!) As with the climbing of Everest, it has all been achieved step by step through the efforts of many men, sometimes many generations. And as far as a means of classification and identification in natural history was concerned, naturalists from Aristotle onwards – through Caspar Bauhin, Gesner, Ray, Joseph Tournefort, Sebastien Vaillant and so on – had all sought a satisfactory method. All had contributed something and from their findings and propositions Linnaeus had profited, especially for example from Ray's *Synopsis methodica animalium quadrupedum et serpentini generis*. Linnaeus's great contribution was that he did bring order into it all.

Linnaeus eventually applied his system to all branches of nature, mammals, birds, fishes, amphibia, insects, minerals, and even diseases. But his primary interest, as with Ray, was botany. Flowers were always easier to study in many respects. You did not have to stalk them, they would not fly away and they were not dangerous, even when attacked! Inspired especially by the suggestions of the French botanist Sebastien Vaillant, Linnaeus demonstrated conclusively that the reproduction of plants had a 'sexual' basis. Pollination was carried out by male and female organs in collaboration, respectively stamens and pistils. Usually these organs were contained in the same plant: in some cases male and female grew on separate plants and had to be brought together or pollinated by external means (which, it was later realized, consisted principally of insects such as bees).

Linnaeus proceeded to arrange his plants according to the number of stamens or male organs for purposes of identification. Those with one stamen became known as Monandria, plants with two stamens were Diandria, and with three stamens Triandria. After ten stamens they were simply classed as 'indefinite' or 'numerous'. As for plants with male and female parts together, they were called Monoecia. Those with male and female parts on separate plants were classed as Dioecia. Altogether Linnaeus divided plants into twenty-four classes, including plants without flowers such as the mosses.

He waxed surprisingly eloquent in describing his findings and referred to 'Floral Nuptials', which was rather startling for such an age:

> The actual petals of a flower contribute nothing to generation, serving only as the bridal bed which the great Creator has so gloriously prepared, adorned with such precious bed-curtains, and perfumed with so many sweet scents in order that the bridegroom and bride may therein celebrate their nuptials with the greater solemnity. When the bed has been made ready, then is the time for the bridegroom to embrace his beloved bride and surrender himself to her.

He talked of one husband in a marriage in the case of a certain plant, two husbands in another and, real polyandry this, 'twenty males or more in the same bed together with the female', and there were many sexual allusions in his attempt to explain the workings of humble flowers. Vast interest was shown in Linnaeus's newfangled sexual system; but there were outraged cries of protest as well. Typical among the latter was Johann Siegesbäck, a St Petersburg professor, who spoke out against Linnaeus's 'loathsome harlotry', his 'lewd and licentious system'. The Creator would never have allowed onions, for example, to indulge in such immorality. Fancy any number of male onions in a bed with a female onion!

As far as naming plants, and all else, was concerned, Linnaeus's method was basically simple. All he really did was to rationalize much of what had been previously attempted. His system of nomenclature consisted of giving two names to each particular object. Up to now scientific names had been cumbersome in the extreme. Some species had been described by as many as half a dozen, even ten adjectives, and in his *Critica botanica* he gives one example of what he damns as 'this appalling diagnosis' – namely, *Arum summis labris degustantes mutos reddens*, which, rendered into English, if it can be so termed, was the Arum-which-strikes-dumb-those-who-do-but-taste-it. It is now more modestly *Arum maculata*, or spotted arum – and less modestly Lords-and-Ladies or the Devil's men and women.

Linnaeus's method amounted, one could say, to giving a surname borne by all members of the same family or genus, *followed* by a Christian name to distinguish the particular species and to which that second part of the

binary name alone belonged. Thus, all the different kinds of rose were 'surnamed' *Rosa*, the 'Christian' name of the dogrose being *canina* and of the Burnet rose *pimpinelli-folia*. Likewise with birds: all the thrush clan was sur-named *Turdus*, but the mistle-thrush had the 'given' name of *viscivorus*, and the song-thrush expressively *musicus*. It was all rather like saying Johnson, Ebenezer, Johnson, James. This binomial system of Linnaeus is still in use, and even though some of the names he adopted have been changed, the principle he prescribed of em-ploying the generic name followed by the specific adjec-tive remains unaltered. A rose may smell as sweet by any name, but it is more interesting if one is able to distinguish one from another.

Hammarby, six miles from Uppsala, was the country estate where Linnaeus settled, for he was professor of botany and medicine at the university for more than thirty years. He built a special museum at Hammarby to house his magnificent collection and library.

As with John Ray, whose love of flowers was stimu-lated by his mother, Linnaeus's interest − passion − star-ted from childhood, indeed must have stemmed from his infancy. His father, a Lutheran pastor in the province of Småland in southern Sweden, was a keen gardener, in fact by way of being a botanist. He had the pleasant whimsy of decorating Carl's cradle with flowers, so that the future cataloguer of God's marvels literally grew up surrounded by tokens of nature. '. . . And if he found that flower in his hand when he awoke − Aye, and what

33

then?' But, to his subsequent chagrin, Pastor Nils Linnaeus could not have been expected to anticipate Coleridge's question! When Carl could walk, the pastor used to take him out into the meadows and give him what amounted to botanical lessons, in the pleasantest way imaginable. Moreover, he saw to it rigorously that Carl learned the names of the flowers. Any lisping forgetfulness was threatened by the discontinuation of the lessons. Far from revulsion, as so many parental good intentions induce, an obsession for naming things took hold of the infant Linnaeus (so learned was he to become,

it seems almost *lèse majesté* to use such an epithet) and never deserted him. After these flowery gambollings, for even Lutheran pastors can sometimes relax, as is evidenced by their frequently large families, came more serious work. The pastor had a large garden and he turned over a small part of this to Carl, who worked sedulously among vegetables and flowers alike.

Perhaps it is not too fanciful to suggest that Carl also

When Linnaeus was a student, Uppsala was too backward to grant a degree. But the situation changed considerably when 'The Prince of Botanists' attained the Chair at the university (pictured here).

GUSTAVIANSKA ACADEMIEN
och des gård.

Fr. Akrelius Sculp.

became plant-conscious because of his surname. The pastor's father, Ingemar Bengtsson, had been a farmer. Nils, after the Scandinavian fashion, had simply been known as Nils Ingemarson, in other words Nils son of Ingemar. But when he went to university he had to take a surname of his own. Now, at the ancestral home there stood a handsome and well-loved lime or linden tree – *lind* in Swedish and *lin* in the Småland dialect. Nils thought of that lime tree when he was deciding on a surname and called himself Linnaeus in memory of it. There is no lack of such family details about the background of Linnaeus, for he wrote no fewer than four autobiographies, either a sign of great self-confidence or of second thoughts.

In spite of significantly strewing Carl's way with flowers, the pastor had not the least wish that botany or natural history should have any part in his son's future career. He had, needless to say, no truck with that most prescient of Jesuit sayings, give me a child until he is seven and you can then do what you like with him. Rather, what's good enough for me is good enough for my son, was this stern Lutheran's motto. He could think of no higher ambition for Carl than that he should enter the Church. Fortunately for science and natural history in particular, he was shattered at the eventual verdict of the grammar school at Väzjö. Carl, his teachers pretty well declared, had turned out a dunce. He might make a living as a tailor or a carpenter or maybe a farm-hand. But assuredly he was not bright enough to reach the dizzy heights of the pulpit.

Not for the first time it was the teachers themselves who had failed to spark off their pupil. But at least one of them, Dr Rothman, had encouraged Carl in his devotion to botany. Simultaneously he aroused in him an interest in medicine – and as we have seen, botany and medicine were still closely linked in many respects. So, to the mortification of his parents (they took it out on their second son, Samuel, and forbade him the pleasures of the garden as a result, whereupon he took to bee-keeping instead), it was decided that Linnaeus should train as a physician. Unfit to become a spiritual guide and comforter, he was considered likely material as a healer. Yet nobody could have been more pious or religious than Linnaeus. He constantly showed this in his awareness of the wonders of the earth.

When one sits [in the meadows at home] in the summer and listens to the cuckoo and the song of all the other birds, the chirping and humming of the insects; when one looks at the shining, gaily coloured flowers, one is completely stunned by the incredible resourcefulness of the Creator.

For the time being, though, Linnaeus threw himself conscientiously into his medical studies. He attended Uppsala University where, he recounts, he was so poor that he had to borrow money for food and clothing. He could not even afford to have his shoes repaired and stuffed them instead with layers of paper. Yet so devoted was he that even when he won a useful little scholarship, he spent the proceeds on a journey to Stockholm. A woman condemned for murder had been hanged and her body had been presented to the College of Medicine. Linnaeus hot-footed it to the capital in order to be present at the dissection.

All this time his passion for nature, and flowers especially, was overpowering everything else. He taught himself more than he was taught, for he records that not once at Uppsala did he hear a single lecture on botany. However, the seed was already there inside him and Linnaeus was furiously active, not merely in botany. Everything interested him. When, for example, he visited the iron-mines at Dannemora, he was just as curious about a 'fire machine' designed by Marten Triewald as the shrew-mice which were so tame they would feed out of people's hands. But he never forsook medicine and eventually practised for a time in Stockholm where he became Professor of Medicine at the university later in his career.

Many of his future works were already germinating, some indeed were being written. A turning-point in Linnaeus's career was undoubtedly his journey of exploration into Lapland, which he undertook in 1732. For Linnaeus this was quite as seminal in its own way as the voyage in the *Beagle* was for Darwin almost exactly a hundred years later.

Nowadays a journey to Lapland sounds mild enough: safari tours to the Land of the Midnight Sun by minibus; an expensive rod on the Tana or the Barduelv; the Lapps using helicopters to visit their herds; snow-mobiles instead of reindeer sleighs. But in those days Lapland was

Hoping to gain useful knowledge about the Earth's shape, the
Frenchman Pierre-Louis Maupertuis, rival of Buffon, made an
expedition to Lapland in 1736–7 and had as tough a time as
Linnaeus. In 1789–91 the Italian Joseph Acerbi was also inspired
to venture there. This plate from Acerbi's book *Travels through
Sweden, Finland and Lapland to the North Cape*, shows Lapp
fishermen sheltering in the smoke from the mosquitoes, while
their catch is cured alongside.

still considered a savage country, cut off by its fearsome climate, its dwarfish inhabitants being regarded with a mixture of contempt and dread, ruled over apparently by shamans who beat out diabolical charms on their magic drums. It was a completely uncharted region, of which there was only rudimentary knowledge in the shape of works such as the sixteenth-century *Historia de gentibus septentrionalibus* of Olaus Magnus and Johann Scheffer's *Lapponia* of 1673. Olof Rudbeck the Younger, one of Linnaeus's mentors, had made a scientific expedition there in 1695, but his material and much else had been tragically lost in the great fire of 1702 which devastated Uppsala – and incidentally caused the subsequent death through sheer grief of Olof Rudbeck the Elder, founder of the Uppsala Botanic Garden for which in his day Linnaeus did so much.

However, the very fact that Lapland was considered such a barbaric, unknown place where nature abounded and the reindeer-herding 'Skrithifinoi' were such curiosities, helped Linnaeus in his application for a grant towards his journey. With his mother's lamentations counterbalanced by his father's prayers, he set off into the virtual unknown.

Having been appointed by the Royal Society of Science to travel through Lapland for the purpose of investigation of the three Kingdoms of Nature there, I prepared my wardrobe and other necessaries for the journey as follows: My clothes consisted of a little unpleated coat of West Gothland cloth with facings and a collar of worsted shag, neat leather breeches, a pig-tailed wig, a cap of green fustian, a pair of top boots, and a small leather bag, nearly two feet long and not quite so wide, with hooks on one side so that it can be shut and hung up. In this bag I carried a shirt, two pairs of half-sleeves, two nightcaps, an ink-horn, a pen-case, a magnifying glass and a small spy-glass, a gauze veil to protect me from midges, this journal and a stock of sheets of paper, stitched together, to press plants between, a comb and my manuscripts on ornithology, my *Flora Uplandica* and *Characteres generici*. A short sword hung at my side, and I had a small fowling-piece between my thigh and the saddle. I had also a graduated eight-sided rod for taking measurements. In my pocket was a wallet containing my

Linnaeus's *Lapland Journal* was full of little sketches: 'When we were on the slopes of Skalka, there appeared in the north-west a gap between the mountains, through which there glared other mountains at a distance of seventy or eighty miles, all white, as if they had not been more than seven miles away.' His words are perhaps more graphic than his drawings.

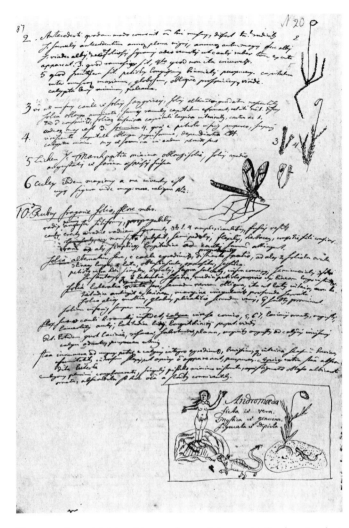

That same journal (pictured here and opposite), conscientiously entered up day after day, often in difficult circumstances, is typical of the pains the naturalists went to in order to preserve the record of their discoveries and observations. They knew only too well that, in Goldsmith's words, 'memory is a fond deceiver'. Accurate and immediate note-taking is a *sine qua non* for the naturalist.

passport from the Governor of Uppsala and a letter of recommendation from the Society. Thus equipped, I left Uppsala on Friday 12 May 1732 at eleven o'clock. I was twenty-five years old, all but about half a day.

His *Tour of Lapland* was not published until the nineteenth century, long after his death. Thanks to the enterprise of Sir James Edward Smith, who acquired much of Linnaeus's material, the manuscript is in the possession of the Linnean Society of London, founded in 1788. It is full of meticulous details, of his daily activities, the flowers he gathered, mileage records, general impressions, all illustrated by his own impromptu sketches, caricatures almost – a Lapp guide transporting a boat on his head during a stretch of porterage to avoid some rapids, a Lapp kota or tent and its construction, a Lapp fish-trap, a Lapp child in its birchlog cradle, reindeer sledges, birds, insects, flowers.

These sketches were of the simplest kind but they sometimes caused a sensation among Lapps to whom he happened to show them. One Laplander was so alarmed at the sight of these drawings, no doubt taking them to be akin to the magic symbols of a shaman's drum, that 'he took off his cap, bowed, and remained with head down and hand on breast as if in veneration, muttering to himself and trembling as if he was about to faint'.

The magic drums mentioned were painted with all manner of secret signs on which metal rings were placed. Then, says Johann Turi in his *Book of Lapland*, the shamans would strike the drums 'with a hammer of copper or horn, and they whistled, and sometimes they ground their teeth. And then they were ready to work magic'. Rather like a game of roulette, everything depended on the signs the rings eventually landed on. Linnaeus tells a gruesome story in this connection which sums up much of the contemporary attitude to Lapland. The Lutheran Church was fanatically eager to eliminate Shamanism and the Lapps were forbidden to use these drums. If a shaman was suspected of secretly possessing one, the Swedish authorities, at the instigation of Lutheran 'missionaries', would seize the man bodily, cut open the main artery in his arm, and leave him to bleed to death. Unless of course in the meantime he accepted the gentle yoke of Christianity.

Linnaeus travelled four thousand miles through the

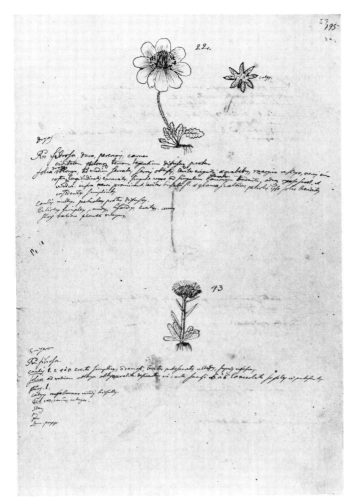

arctic wilds, sometimes on horseback, sometimes on foot, sometimes by boat. He tells us how he struggled knee-deep through bogs, and waist-deep through icy torrents. He was frequently on the verge of starvation, frequently in danger of his life as when his boat capsized and was smashed to smithereens on the rocks. At times he despaired and thought the hardships he underwent would have been too cruel a punishment even for a capital crime. 'How I wished that I had never undertaken my journey.'

The Lapland journey was undoubtedly a considerable achievement, both in itself and for its results. But, out of vanity or the hope of extracting more money from the Royal Society of Science by wringing their withers, Linnaeus does seem to have drawn the long bow at times.

In her book *The Prince of Botanists* Norah Gourlie has pointed out various factual misstatements, including one claim which if true would have meant Linnaeus had averaged sixty miles a day during one period of the journey.

He had no need to exaggerate, even supposing he had done so. His journey to that far country was almost as sensational in his age as space travel has been in our day.

6 Music for the Master

Linnaeus had not truly relished his Lapland adventures and was thankful to return to 'civilization'. In future his travels were to be more sedate. As for obtaining specimens and material, he subsequently employed some of his more devoted students to go to the ends of the earth on his behalf.

Nevertheless, Lapland helped to make his name. He returned to Uppsala in triumph, with much material and great inspiration for his future work. He was extremely proud of his Lapland enterprise and used to sport a Lapp costume as he strutted through the town. He even donned it some years later when he was courting the girl who became his wife. And he did not fail to take it with him, together with a shaman's drum, when presently he visited Germany, Holland and England.

Usually, though, that picturesque souvenir hung on a wall of his work-room, which became a museum in miniature. It was crammed with rare books, scientific instruments, rare plants in pots, rock samples, an array of shellfish, a large collection of insects and literally thousands of pressed flowers and other botanical items, while placed in one corner were the branches of a tree on which thirty different kinds of tame birds perched themselves. Everything in this scientific workshop was arranged according to the new system Linnaeus had evolved.

Immediately after his return from Lapland he was mainly occupied in writing his *Flora Lapponica*, and he also read various papers to the Royal Society of Science with such unexpected titles as 'The Cause of Cattle Death in Tornea'. But this man of many parts was not content with botany or Lapland: he found time to develop his interest in mineralogy, concerning which he wanted to familiarize himself with assaying. He admitted knowing next to nothing on the subject, but, acting on the principle that the best way to learn about something is to teach someone else, he took to lecturing on assaying and even compiled a successful handbook on it. Here was a typical example of Linnean self-confidence.

It is often said that scientists, brilliant though they may be, are frequently unable to communicate in a lucid way. Both John Ray and Linnaeus refute this contention by their admirable style of writing. Linnaeus provides us with a vivid illustration of his descriptive powers in his account of a visit to a famous copper-mine in the Falun region of central Sweden.

We went the whole way down by wooden ladders, mostly of twenty rungs each, hanging vertically and free of the wall. Often they were joined in pairs and only supported at their ends, so that they swayed about. Down below the drifts were so low that we had to stoop or crawl, and so narrow that many a time we had to turn our bodies sideways in order to move forward; again and again I knocked my head on projecting bits of the roof – a roof that was covered with crystallized vitriol of a curious blackish colour. All the men carried torches in their mouths. At the bottom there blew a cold wind strong enough to turn a windmill. The horses which drew the winch were driven by a man who stood close to the axle, and there were stalls, hay and a smithy. The ore was carried in wheelbarrows or small four-wheeled waggons.

In these gloomy places to which no daylight ever penetrates, these doomed creatures – there were about twelve hundred of them – lived and had their being; yet they seemed to be content, because they fought to get jobs there. They are surrounded on every hand by rock and gravel, by dripping corrosive vitriol, by smoke, steam, heat and dust. There is a constant risk of sudden death from the collapse of a roof, so that they can never feel safe for a single second. The great depth, the dark and the danger, made my hair stand on end with fright, and I wished for one thing only – to be back again on the surface. These wretched men live by the sweat of their brows, working naked to the waist and with a woollen rag tied over their mouths to prevent them so far as possible from inhaling fumes and dust. The sweat poured from them like water from a bag. It was only too easy to fall into a hole, to miss one's footing on the rung of a ladder; or a rock might come crashing down and kill some miserable man instantly. Every aspect of hell was there for me to see.

Apart from the fact that Zola would have rubbed our noses in it much more, that passage might have come from *Germinal*.

The visit to Falun came about through Linnaeus's friendship with one of his pupils, Claes Sohlberg, whose father was an inspector of mines. Now, the standard of Swedish universities at that time was not notably high

This title-page commemorates the names of Hermann Boerhaave, the Dutch biologist and physician, and Sir J.E. Smith, into whose hands the book came as part of Linnaeus's collection. Boerhaave found the Swede somewhat conceited but put him in touch with patrons to finance his work. Linnaeus records Boerhaave's habit of raising his hat to any elder tree he passed out of respect for its medicinal qualities.

and Sohlberg suggested to Linnaeus that he should take Claes to Holland as part of his tutorial duties. The Golden Age of the Netherlands, typified by Franz Hals and Vermeer and Rembrandt, had of course long since passed, but the Dutch were still enjoying a brilliant and affluent period. Their extensive empire had reached into the Far East and broadened their horizons both metaphorically and actually. The wild treasure-house of the East Indies had stimulated their interest in nature.

Linnaeus had no patience for superstitious frauds. In addition to debunking the Hamburg hydra, he showed that certain bones preserved in a church as the remains of a giant came from a whale.

In spite of the continual scientific ferment that was taking place (it was after all an age when, for example, John Hadley had invented the navigational sextant, when Boerhaave was establishing the science of organic chemistry and Claudius Aymand carried out the first successful operation for appendicitis), there is an amusing incident during Linnaeus's journey to Holland that shows how credulity had still not been vanquished. Because of foul weather and the difficulty of obtaining onward passage, Linnaeus and his pupil were forced to linger awhile in Germany, including a visit to Hamburg.

The burgomaster of that city possessed a famous seven-headed hydra, a monster that had originally been acquired a hundred years earlier from the altar of a pillaged church in Prague. It was now an extremely valuable curiosity and even the Danish king had tried to purchase it. To the chagrin of the burgomaster, Linnaeus proceeded to emulate, though in a less arduous way, Hercules, who, with the aid of Iolas, had destroyed the original hydra. Linnaeus simply demolished the Hamburg hydra with one glance of his famous sharp-sighted brown eyes. He at once pronounced it as a ridiculous fake. The jaws and claws of the 'monster' had been cleverly made up from the remains of weasels and the main body was covered with snake-skins stuck together. When Hercules was destroying *his* hydra, Juno, jealous of his glory, sent a large crab to bite his foot. Perhaps fearing the equivalent from the furious burgomaster, whose once valuable property was now worthless, Linnaeus hurriedly moved on.

Linnaeus was always fortunate in the friendships he made. At Uppsala he had been greatly helped by Dr Olof Celsius, who, impressed by Linnaeus's obvious genius in botany, sheltered and fed him and put his garden and library at his disposal. Olof was the uncle of Anders Celsius, the astronomer and inventor of the thermometer that bears his name. At Uppsala too Linnaeus had become deeply attached to Peter Artedi who, building on the work of John Ray and Francis Willughby and their *Historia piscium*, became one of the leading ichthyologists of the time. Indeed, some have called him the 'father' of that branch of natural history. Artedi met a tragic death – as it happened, when Linnaeus was in Holland – by drowning in one of Amsterdam's canals, into which he fell one evening the worse for too much wine. The two friends had sworn a pact that, in the event of either's death, the survivor would regard it as a sacred duty to see that the other's work was not lost to the world. With the help of a generous Englishman, Linnaeus honoured that pact and saw to the publication of Artedi's work. He undoubtedly owed a great debt to Artedi in his own classification work. Artedi's direct influence on Linnaeus cannot be exaggerated. Linnaeus called him the ornament and glory of his country.

Apart from that tragedy, which entailed a serious loss to natural history, Linnaeus's stay in Holland was pleasant enough. The Dutch naturalist Johan Gronovius was so impressed by his *Systema naturae* that, knowing

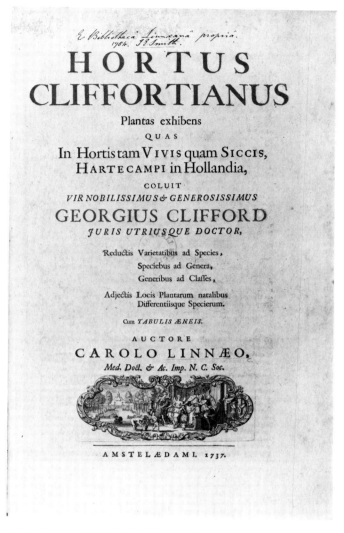

Again, the name of J.E. Smith can be seen at the top of this catalogue Linnaeus made of the botanical collection at Hartecamp belonging to his 'most noble and most generous' patron, George Clifford.

Periodically an outcry is raised (and occasionally funds also) when a famous work of art is in danger of being sold to a foreign buyer. But the Elgin marbles, consisting of the sculptures of Pheidias, were brought to England from Greece. And Sir J.E. Smith (pictured above) got hold of the Linnean Collection.

(Opposite) After their voyage in the seductive tropics, Banks and Solander went to another extreme – botanizing in Iceland. Banks must have found home life in Iceland (pictured right) somewhat different from the glamour of Tahiti.

knighted. Smith, one of the many amateur naturalists of the day, had for long been an ardent champion of Linnaeus.

Linnaeus's collection grew increasingly during his illustrious career, so that he had been obliged to build a special museum for it on his estate at Hammarby. When he died in 1778, his property, including his vast library, equally vast collection and many unpublished papers, went to his son, also named Carl. This Carl only survived his father by five years, and his widow, afraid of losing the collection to the rest of Carl's family, put it up for sale. Such was the fame of the Linnaeus Collection that even Catherine II, Empress of Russia, considered buying it.

However, Smith, encouraged by Sir Joseph Banks, got in first with his offer. Rich enough for such an enterprise, he chartered an English ship, the *Appearance*, to transport the booty to England. It is said, perhaps apochryphally, that when the Swedes came to and realized what they were losing, they sent a warship in pursuit and there were even contemporary cartoons drawn of this abortive chase. Be that as it may, Smith safely brought his treasure trove home, tens of thousands of pressed plants, thousands of insects, shells, mineral specimens, thousands of books, letters, manuscripts. In 1778, on the basis of this haul, the Linnean Society of London was founded, and it remains one of the most respected natural history bodies in the world. Appropriately enough James Edward Smith was its first president.

That of course is anticipating events. The fame of Linnaeus had become even greater through his journeys abroad, for it gave his contemporaries a better chance to appreciate his genius and his astonishing range. On his return to Sweden, particularly after he took the chair of botany at Uppsala, students flocked to listen to his lectures. One of the activities Linnaeus came to enjoy during his later years was taking parties of students, sometimes as many as two or three hundred, into the Swedish countryside on nature expeditions. They would be split up into smaller groups, each with a leader armed with a bugle. As soon as anything remarkable was found, a rare plant or unusual bird, the bugle was sounded to summon everyone to the spot. At the end of the day, the whole party would march back to town in triumph, headed by a makeshift band in symbolic honour of the Master. Bird-watching cruises round the Hebrides or safari trips to Serengeti are nowadays common enough. They have grown from the example set by Carolus Linnaeus two hundred years ago, even if they have dispensed with the band.

Some of the students moved on to far more arduous and more dangerous enterprises than pottering about the flowery environs of Uppsala. Linnaeus, as we have indicated, had had his fill of perilous travel in Lapland. In future his hardships were to be suffered by proxy. To advance the cause of botany, he encouraged and trained many of his devoted student-disciples to travel infinitely farther afield. Africa, South America, India, Ceylon, Japan, Tahiti, New Zealand – they went to the ends of the earth at the behest of the Master. And many of them

left their bones there, in days when the 'white man's grave' was not confined to West Africa.

It was this aspect of the Linnean field that inspired a man such as Philibert de Commerson to go plant-hunting in the Pacific with Louis de Bougainville. 'Glory requires, like Fortune, a race of men both hardy and tenacious,' Commerson wrote, and for this fanatical botanist, glory consisted in discovering exotic flowers and bringing them back to France where Louis XV had appointed him Royal Botanist. But the most striking example abroad of Linnaeus's influence was Banks (in a letter to the naturalist John Ellis, Linnaeus later returned the compliment by referring to the 'immortal' Banks). The Englishman's admiration for Linnaeus led him directly to persuade the British authorities to allow Banks, together with Daniel Solander, Linnaeus's most

The best-known 'likeness' of Sir Joseph Banks was by Reynolds, and this bust of him shows him as an elder statesman of the scientific world. As a young man he was a lively character. In the Pacific he harboured an uninhibited admiration for the Polynesian beauties, particularly a girl named Otiatia, by whom he had a child.

(Opposite above) An elephant with unlikely three-toed feet from Pliny's *Historia naturalis* (Nicholas Jenson, 1476). In fact, the African elephant has three nails on its rounded hind feet, four on the front; the Indian elephant an extra one in each case.

(Opposite below) Pliny in his study, from the same edition. He had a vast capacity for work, much of which he did at night. Even while he was being rubbed down after a bath, he would have a book read to him or would dictate notes.

experienced student-collector, to accompany Captain James Cook on his voyage of circumnavigation in the years 1768–71. The fact that Banks was a wealthy man with estates in Yorkshire, which enabled him to put up £10,000 towards the expedition, no doubt helped, but he was already an experienced traveller through his journey to Newfoundland.

Sir Joseph Banks was the prototype of the wealthy dilettante. Yet although he has been dubbed the Grand Cham of the natural history circles of his time, he was brilliant in his own right. He was President of the Royal Society for forty-three years, an illustrious successor to Sir Hans Sloane and just as avid a collector. His house in Soho Square was always a lively meeting-place for men of science in general, and there was an open welcome for the humblest scientific contribution either in the form of verbal information or an item for Sir Joseph's immense collection. He was lavish in his patronage and had, for example, sponsored Mungo Park in his Nigerian travels. He employed successively Solander, another Swedish botanist, Jonas Dryander, and Robert Brown to take charge of his magnificent library. At his own expense he employed Francis Bauer, who (with his brother Ferdinand) was perhaps the most accomplished botanical artist of the time.

Banks's interest in botany started at Eton (whither he moved from Harrow!), not through any formal lessons he was able to obtain on the subject, but from 'cullers of simples', as he termed them – women with a knowledge of the use of herbs whom he paid sixpence a time for any worthwhile plants they brought him. Later on, thanks to living in Chelsea, he was able to make extensive use of the botanical garden of the Apothecaries' Company. It was in the sphere of botanical collecting that Banks was especially skilled. He took over control of the Royal Gardens at Kew and raised them to a position of pre-eminence in the botanical world. And he laid the groundwork for the Hookers, father and son, which they built on so successfully.

One of the schemes he put into operation on behalf of Kew was in the full Linnean tradition. He trained collectors to travel world-wide to bring back exotic plants. At least he knew plenty about the hazards and discomforts involved through his travels with Cook. He cheerfully warned his 'young men' that there was an even

chance of their being shipwrecked, dying of snake-bite or fever, if they did not end up in the cooking-pot of cannibals with a taste for 'long pig'.

Banks had a fertile mind: he saw the inherent possibilities in india-rubber; he was the first to advocate tea plantations in India. It was he, too, who conceived the idea of fetching bread-fruit from Tahiti for planting as food for slaves in the sugar plantations of the West Indies. He sent out one of his most talented collectors, David Nelson, with the famous, or infamous, *Bounty* expedition for the purpose of obtaining the bread-fruit. After the mutiny, Nelson stuck by Captain Bligh during his fearful open-boat voyage of forty-seven days and 4,500 miles, but he died in agony of lung-fever at the end of it. Another of Sir Joseph's protégés, the gardener-botanist William Brown, joined the mutineers and sailed with Fletcher Christian to Pitcairn. He ended up with a musket-shot in his back from one of the discontented Tahitians.

Banks's *Journal*, written 'during Captain Cook's First Voyage in H.M.S. Endeavour' was, at least in its original version, even racy in parts. For though one of the objects of the expedition was to observe the transit of Venus, Sir Joseph was keenly interested in the more earthbound Venuses of Tahiti of whom he was clearly, and understandably, fond. However, Joseph Hooker edited it for Victorian readers to such an extent that it has been described as 'not so much a journal as a piece of carnage'.

Even so, the journal is crammed with material far more lively than many a novel of the time, whether Banks is describing a wrestling-match, the theft of a precious astronomical quadrant and the ensuing chase after the thief, or merely a certain flowery inlet, 'which appeared to be very good', and where he observed

. . . four small canoes, each containing one man, who held in his hand a long pole, with which he struck fish, venturing with his little embarkation almost into the surf. These people seemed to be totally engaged in what they were about: the ship passed within a quarter of a mile of them, and yet they scarcely lifted their eyes from their employment. I was almost inclined to think that, attentive to their business and deafened by the noise of the surf, they neither saw nor heard her go past.

(Opposite) *The Pelican in her Piety* was reputed to nourish her young ones with her own blood. In fact, they almost disappear in the enormous pouch for regurgitated food. From the fourteenth-century *Bestiare d'Amour* by Richard de Fournivall.

Of New Zealanders Captain Cook wrote, 'some are punctured or stained in the face with curious spiral and other figures, of a black or deep blue colour'.

But those preoccupied aboriginal fishermen were not to be left in peace for long. Banks named that arcadian inlet Botany Bay and he recommended it to the British Government as an eminently suitable penal settlement. The hulks became full to overflowing when convicts could no longer be dumped in America.

7 'Thou Knowest of No Strange Continent . . .'

He went riding and boating and skating whenever he could. He was an enthusiastic shot, expert enough to bring down snipe, that most elusive of targets. He often danced late into the night. He was variously described as being indolent, procrastinating, and leading a 'rantipole'★ existence. He was never happier than in the company of pretty women, to whom he dedicated some of his bucolic poems. He wrote also of other interests.

I have procured some of the mice mentioned in my former letter, a young one and a female with young, both of which I have preserved in brandy. From the colour, shape, size and manner of nesting, I make no doubt but that the species is nondescript.† They are much smaller and more slender than the *mus domesticus medius* of Ray; and have more of the squirrel or dormouse colour; their belly is white; a straight line along their sides divides the shades of their back and belly. They never enter into houses; are carried into ricks and barns with the sheaves; abound in harvest; and build their nests amidst the straws of the corn above the ground, and sometimes in thistles. They breed as many as eight at a litter, in a little round nest composed of the blades of grass or wheat.

One of these nests I procured this autumn, most artificially plaited, and composed of the blades of wheat; perfectly round, and about the size of a cricket-ball; with the aperture so ingeniously closed that there was no discovering to what part it belonged. It was so compact and well-filled, that it would roll across the table without being discomposed, though it contained eight little mice that were naked and blind. As this nest was perfectly full, how could the dam come at her litter respectively so as to administer a teat to each? Perhaps she opens different places for that purpose, adjusting them again when the business is over: but she could not possibly be contained herself in the ball with her young, which moreover would be daily increasing in bulk. This wonderful procreant cradle, an elegant instance of the effort of instinct, was found in a wheatfield suspended in the head of a thistle.

Return, blithe maidens; with you bring along
Free, native humour, all the charms of song;
The feeling heart, and unaffected ease,
Each nameless grace, and ev'ry power to please. . . .

★Defined in the *Shorter Oxford English Dictionary* as 'a romp; a wild, ill-behaved, reckless person'.
†i.e. not hitherto described.

This sketch of Gilbert White is one of the few likenesses of him. Possibly the only portrait of him now hangs at The Wakes, and even its authenticity is not certain. But White is limned indelibly in his book.

'The village of Selborne, and large hamlet of Oakhanger, with the single farms, and many scattered houses along the verge of the forest, contain upwards of six hundred and seventy inhabitants. We abound with poor, many of whom are sober and industrious, and live comfortably in good stone or brick cottages, which are glazed, and have chambers above stairs: mud buildings we have none.' There are interesting items about contemporary life in that passage.

Surely there must be a mistake here? We can't be talking about one and the same person, who on the one hand could pen lovelorn verses to his favourite beauties and on the other describe in precise, vivid terms the newly discovered harvest mouse! But yes; this was the Reverend Gilbert White, who had more influence in bringing ordinary people to a love and understanding of nature than did many of the giants, such as Linnaeus or Darwin, regarded in the eyes of science as towering far above this modest country parson. There were no exotic journeys for Gilbert White: he never embarked on deeper water than the Thames, never left his native land, spending most of his life in the Hampshire village where he was born. For that matter, he never possessed such paraphernalia as telescope or microscope. Yet by his superb, clear-eyed observation, his loving curiosity in all things and his unconscious ability to impart his enthusiasm to others through his lucid style (in an age fond of literary pomposities), he has earned the gratitude of many generations since.

(Opposite) Being Proctor and Dean of Oriel College could not have been a very arduous post. But it helped provide Gilbert White with financial stability – and pleasant surroundings when he visited Oxford. His table and chair can still be seen at the College.

'To the north-west, north and east of the village, is a range of fair enclosures, consisting of what is called a white malm, a sort of rotten or rubble stone, which, when turned up to frost and rain, moulders and becomes manure in itself. This soil produces good wheat and clover.'

Gilbert White was born on 18 July 1720 at Selborne vicarage, his paternal grandfather being parson of that village. His father, John White, was a barrister who was spared the tediousness of earning a living by prudently marrying an heiress. Perhaps that was where some of Gilbert's alleged indolence and lack of ambition derived. On the other hand, precious little affluence did, for later in life, in connection with the hoped-for renewal of a fellowship, Gilbert had to explain to an Oxford provost that his patrimony amounted to no more than sixty-six pounds, one shilling and fourpence.

In the Whites' different homes in Surrey and Sussex, many brothers and sisters of Gilbert were subsequently born and many died. For it was still an age of large families counterbalanced by great infant mortality. When Gilbert was nine, his parents moved back to Sel-

borne; not to the vicarage, for Parson White was dead, but to the house still called The Wakes, where the vicar's widow was living. The Wakes was, in varying degrees, to be White's home until his death in 1793 and continues to be redolent of his spirit, for it is now the Gilbert White Museum, a place of pilgrimage for thousands of people every year.

Strangely little is known about White's boyhood, except that he went to Basingstoke Grammar School. When he was twenty he was admitted to Oriel College, Oxford, and from then on the picture becomes clearer. This is largely thanks to the principal friend he made there, John Mulso. For John Mulso, who later became a canon of Winchester (enjoying the patronage of his uncle, the Bishop), not only corresponded regularly with Gilbert throughout his life but constantly encouraged

The Wakes, Gilbert White's beloved home from which he hardly stirred in forty years. On one side he planted lime trees to screen the view and reduce the smell of the butcher's shop on the Plestor, centre of the village. The bees would have been grateful for the limes.

him to persevere with the *Natural History and Antiquities of Selborne*, that gentle piece of literary immortality that has appeared in as many editions as there are years since its author's death. Indeed, in one of his letters, Canon Mulso forecast that very immortality.

Evidently life at Oxford was exceedingly pleasurable and bore few signs of Gilbert White's quiet round at Selborne in later years. Apart from the sporting activities mentioned earlier, the correspondence of the two friends is full of significant allusions: 'I never met in one place such an assembly of Beauties. I believe I saved my heart by the beautiful confusion'; 'I would not advise you to play so much as you do with the tangles of Neaera's hair'; 'Has a certain Jenny resumed her Empire and totally expelled her rival?' White was nicknamed 'Busser' by his companions at Oxford ('We busse our wantons, but our wives we kisse', as Robert Herrick put it some eighty years before).

Yet Gilbert White never married. Perhaps it was not so much a question of safety in numbers as his being bemused by them, or maybe he took seriously Mulso's

Year Selborne.	Place. Soil	Therm⁹	Barom⁹	Wind.	Inches of Rain or Sn. Size of Hail ft.	Weather	Trees firſt in leaf. —Fungi firſt appear	Plants firſt in flower Moſses vegetate.	Birds and Inſects firſt appear, or regard to fiſh, and disappear	Obſervations with regard to fiſh, and other animals	Miſcellaneous Obſervations, and Memorandums
Sunday 8 / 12 / June 9. 4 / 8			29 7-10.	S.W.		ſun & clouds. fine even. cool.			early orange lilies blow. few chafers.		
Monday 8 / 12 / 10. 4 / 8			29 7-10½	S.W. W. 16.		ſhowers. cool. gleams. cold air.			Cut five cucumbers.		
Tueſday 8 / 12 / 11. 4 / 8		61.	29 6-10½	S.W.		grey. ſun. louring.			A man brought me a large plate of straw-berries, which were crude, & not near ripe.		
Wednes 8 / 12 / 12. 4 / 8		62.	29 7-10.	N.		bright. ſun. golden even.			cut eight cucumbers. Mrs Clement & children left us. Many swifts.		
Thurf 8 / 12 / 13. 4 / 8		61.	29 8-10½	NE.		ſhower. ſun & cold wind.			cut ten cucumbers. Provence roses blow against a wall. Dames violets very fine. ten weeks Stocks ſtill in full beauty.		
Friday 8 / 12 / 14. 4 / 8		48.	29 8-10.	NE.		cold wind. dark. gleams.			cut four cucumbers. Mr John Mulso came.		
Saturday 8 / 12 / 15. 4 / 8		60.	29 8-10.	NE. W.		cold dew. ſun. louring.			Men wash their ſheep. Mr J. Mulso left us.		

A page from White's *The Naturalist's Journal*. Nothing was too insignificant for him to record, from trout snatching newly hatched mayfly to the appearance of the first meadow saffron.

reference to 'the dreary and dolourous land of matrimony' – though eventually the future canon was to enter that very land. Perhaps, too, there were economic reasons, for had Gilbert married he would have been obliged to relinquish the fellowship which Oriel College now granted him. This, with the benefice of various curacies after he was ordained in 1749, and a junior proctorship at Oxford, formed the bulk of his income.

Besides, for several years to come he enjoyed his freedom. He suffered from coach-sickness and in addition coach travel was relatively expensive (Parson Woodforde, White's contemporary, grumbled that for the inside places in the London to Norwich coach he paid one pound sixteen shillings and that excess baggage cost him eight shillings and sixpence). So Gilbert travelled on horseback – to Essex, in connection with a will of which he was executor (for which his fee was £20), to Glouces-

tershire, Devonshire, Lancashire, and between Oxford and the Hampshire village of Swarraton, where briefly he was curate to his uncle. This leisurely riding along downland tracks, through ferny woods, across rippling fords of a sparsely populated land (the population of England and Wales rose from about 5½ million in Queen Anne's time to 9 million at the turn of the century) must have been an idyllic progress, helping to stimulate White's love of the countryside.

In addition, although he did not take up permanent residence in Selborne until 1755 or inherit The Wakes directly until 1763, he always had it as a pleasant resting-place from his wanderings. He took to living there increasingly, partly because his father became too infirm to manage his affairs and the small 'farmery', and White always had a keen interest in and knowledge of agriculture. Various curacies kept him going: at Faringdon, Berkshire, at West Dean near Salisbury, Wiltshire, while an absentee living at Moreton Pinkney in Northamptonshire brought him in some £30 per annum, but he had to keep a curate there. If he had followed the advice of

Mulso in those days of pluralism he could have waxed fatter.

In spite of his limited means and his developing interest in natural history, Gilbert White continued to enjoy human companionship to the full: 'Drank tea twenty of us at the Heritage [a thatched shelter he had built in the grounds of The Wakes]: the Misses Batties and the Mulso family contributed much to our pleasure by their singing and being dressed as shepherds and shepherdesses. It was a most elegant evening; and all parties appeared highly satisfied.' While one of those same Misses Battie recorded that 'we kept it up with mirth and jollity. The morning was spent at the Harpsichord; a Ball at night began with minuets at half an hour after seven, then country dances till near eleven when we went to supper and afterwards sat down some time, sang, laughed, talked and then went to dancing again till three in the morning'.

And why shouldn't the portrait of this naturalist let in a glimpse of the sunlight that constantly irradiated his life, whether he was wearing fancy dress in the ballroom, or watching the bees pollinate his cucumbers, or tending his hops and vines, or simply caring for his parishioners? As to the last activity, it could well have been this, in part at least, that gave rise to suggestions of indolence. Mulso in later years often railed at White for the slow progress he was making in completing his *Natural History* for publication. But for all his devotion to nature, it was White's duty as priest that always came first, not simply church services, weddings, baptisms and burials, but visiting people and helping the needy. ('A petticoat for Tull's naked wench,' we read; 'a warm waistcoat for old Lee'.)

His serious nature writings started in a desultory fashion. In 1751 he began to keep a diary, or *Garden Kalendar* as he called it. This included both nature and gardening notes and also entries about his social activities such as we have read above. The *Garden Kalendar* soon gave way to *The Naturalist's Journal*. This was a new day-book devised by the Honourable Daines Barrington for the purpose of recording nature notes (in itself an interesting sidelight on the times) and published by Gilbert's younger brother Benjamin of the publishing firm of B. White & Son, London.

In the meantime, Benjamin White had suggested to Thomas Pennant that his firm should publish a new edition of Pennant's *British Zoology*, originally brought out in 1761, with four more editions up to 1812. It was through this publishing connection that Gilbert White met Pennant. Subsequently their long-lasting acquaintance was continued through correspondence, for Pennant lived in North Wales.

Pennant was a highly talented zoologist, though of the 'closet' variety as Charles Waterton would have dubbed him, a collector and sifter of information but not a field naturalist. He immediately recognized Gilbert White's worth as a true and accurate observer of nature. In the years to come, Pennant was to make frequent use of White, asking him specifically to study a certain species and report on it to him or even gather specimens for the guidance of his illustrator. Subsequent editions of *British Zoology* and also the *History of Quadrupeds* (1781) owed much to White's ready information. But even though Pennant may have been quite ulterior in his motives, we must be thankful for the fact that it was his acquaintanceship with White that contributed greatly to the eventual compilation of the latter's *Natural History of Selborne*.

The other fruitful correspondence Gilbert White conducted was with Daines Barrington, lawyer, antiquarian, writer, amateur naturalist and member of the Royal Society. White's letters to Pennant and Barrington constitute respectively the two halves of the book.

Dear Sir, [he writes to Pennant on 27 July 1768] . . . A person by my order has searched our brooks, but could find no such fish as the *gasterosteus pungitius*:★ he found the *gasterosteus aculeatus*† in plenty. This morning, in a basket, I packed a little earthen pot full of wet moss, and in it some sticklebacks, male and female; the females big with spawn: some lamperns; some bulls heads; but I could procure no minnows. This basket will be in Fleet Street by eight this evening; so I hope Mazel the engraver will have them fresh and fair tomorrow morning. I gave some directions, in a letter, to what particulars he should be attentive.

(Opposite) The great bat or noctule could fitly be called White's bat, for it was Gilbert White who first called attention to it as a native British species. He called it *Altovolans* because 'it ranges very high for its food, feeding in a different region of the air'. Of the honey buzzard he wrote: 'When on the wing this species may be easily distinguished from the common buzzard by its hawklike appearance, small head, wings not so blunt, and longer tail.'

★Ten-spined stickleback. †Three-spined stickleback.

GREAT BAT.

HONEY-BUZZARD.

A HYBRID BIRD.
Published at the Act directs by J. White, Jan.y 1.st 1802.
VOL. II. page 123.

From an edition of Gilbert White's book and almost a caricature of the lifeless specimens nature artists used as models in the days before Audubon revolutionized methods of depicting wild creatures.

Dear Sir, [he writes to Barrington]

Your observation that the cuckoo does not deposit its egg indiscriminately in the nest of the first bird that comes its way, but probably looks out a nurse in some degree congenerous, with whom to entrust its young, is perfectly new to me; and struck me so forcibly that I naturally fell into a train of thought that led me to consider whether the fact was so, and what reason there was for it. When I came to recollect and inquire, I could not find that any cuckoo had ever been seen in these parts except in the nest of the wagtail, the hedge-sparrow, the titlark, the white-throat, and the red-breast, all soft-billed insectivorous birds.

Nothing was too lowly for his interest. He wrote eloquently about earthworms (foreshadowing Darwin's last work a century later, *On the Formation of Mould through the Action of Worms*), pointing out that though seemingly a 'small and despicable link in the chain of Nature', they were of immeasurable importance. Apart from the fact that many birds and mammals depended on them for food, worms carried out an immensely important function in promoting the aeration and general refinement of the soil.

It was his perceptiveness about earthworms that brought him to a knowledge, incomplete though it might be in modern terms, of what we call ecology. White, of course, never used the word which was not to come into currency for another hundred years: he called it the 'Oeconomy of Nature'. But he certainly knew what it was all about. He ponders for example how certain beans could have arrived in a place far from normal cultivation. Too far for mice to have carried them, he concludes: they must have been transported by birds. Those wagtails running about in the neighbourhood of grazing cows: clearly they were profiting from the insects pestering the animals. Similarly, a crowd of swallows diving and swooping in the wake of horsemen were feeding on the flies disturbed by the passing hoofs.

He observed that similarities in the appearance of different creatures did not mean that they led the same kind of life or even lived in the same habitat. House crickets preferred the glowing warmth of hearth or ovenside, but field crickets preferred dry, sunny banks. Yet another member of the genus, the mole-cricket, worked and lived in a completely different way, enabled by its peculiar forefeet to burrow almost like a mole – to the great detriment of garden beds.

Again, creatures of different species that consumed the same kind of food, did so in different ways. The nuthatch, the squirrel and the field-mouse, he wrote in Letter LVI to Daines Barrington, all have a taste for hazel-nuts. The squirrel, after rasping off the small end, splits the shell in two with its long foreteeth, as a man does with a knife. The nuthatch, having no paws to hold the nut firm while he pierces it, fixes it as it were in a vice, 'like an adroit workman', in a cleft of the tree. As for the field-mouse, he simply 'nibbles a hole with his teeth, so regular as if drilled with a wimble [gimlet], and yet so small that one wonders how it can extract the kernel'.

Sometimes he had his doubts. He accepted Linnaeus's opinion that swallows hibernated: 'A Swedish naturalist is so much persuaded of that fact, that he talks, in his calendar of *Flora*, as familiarly of the swallow's going under water in the beginning of September, as he would

of his poultry going to roost a little before sunset.' But he then qualified this comment by suggesting that though they might not actually retire underwater for the winter, they might conceal themselves in the banks of pools and rivers during the 'uncomfortable' months. Why otherwise did they congregate in reed-banks in early autumn? However, he changed his mind about swallows when he received news from his brother John, chaplain to the garrison of Gibraltar, of large numbers of the birds passing that way at set times of the year.

When he was sure about something, he said so; even to the extent of correcting the great man himself. Linnaeus opined that the cuckoo was a bird of prey, taken in no doubt by certain superficial resemblances to a sparrowhawk. (The present writer remembers, a good many years ago, gamekeepers who were convinced that the cuckoo turned into a hawk in winter and so took the precautions one would expect of them.) This is not so, affirmed White. The cuckoo is no raptor; Linnaeus was wrong.

But he did not tell Linnaeus so himself. He was too modest. It was his brother John who, somewhat pompously, corresponded with Linnaeus – on the basis of material that Gilbert had passed on to him. John rather fancied himself as a zoologist, though even his brother Benjamin did not think highly enough of his 'Fauna of Gibraltar' to publish it.

Gilbert White was too modest also to apply for membership of the Royal Society and it was Daines Barrington who read to that august body White's papers on swallows, martins and swifts – monographs which were subsequently published in the Society's *Philosophical Transactions*. None the less, White did at least have the satisfaction of seeing his *Natural History* published in 1788, five years before his death. Its eventual and continuing success is too well known to need recounting. But its reception at the outset was, with a few exceptions, cautious, even condescending in some cases. This was perhaps partly owing to the fact that Gilbert White had no professional training as a zoologist, which must have displeased some of the more jealous pundits. Nor was he a self-publicist, as to some extent Linnaeus was. He much preferred wandering along the Zig-zag and Bostal paths of his beloved Hanger, identifying a 'new' warbler, or entertaining his numerous nephews and nieces at The

Wakes rather than seeking fame in London.

It is indeed Gilbert White's simplicity and modesty that have endeared him to so many ordinary people, together with his infectious enthusiasm and his demonstration that there was always something new to be discovered in nature if you looked with a sharp eye and a loving one. He was far more concerned with the living world – the territorial implications of bird-song, the hunting methods of the bat, the sagacity of a willow-wren in scattering moss over its nest to hide its brood – than with the sedulous, albeit necessary classification and dissection that obsessed others.

However, all this would have counted for far less but for one other factor: his marvellously clear and unpretentious style of writing, a model not always followed by more professional zoologists. One of the most favourable contemporary reviews, which appeared in *The Topographer*, sums it all up:

Brueghel with his paintings, Vivaldi with his music, John Clare with his poetry – many have been the interpreters of country life. To us, Gilbert White's times seem romantic enough, but not all the rural scene was as pretty as the proverbial picture.

A more delightful or more original work than Mr White's *History of Selborne* has seldom been published. The book is not a compilation from former publications, but the result of many years' attentive observations of nature itself, which are told not only with the precision of a philosopher, but with that happy selection of circumstances, which mark the poet. Throughout therefore not only the understanding is informed, but the imagination is touched. And, if the criterion of excellence, that Dr Johnson, I think, somewhere in the lives of the poets, proposes as true, Mr White's book is excellent, for I beheld the end of it with the pensive regret with which a traveller looks upon the setting sun.

8 'Bless the Squire'

The skein of pink-footed geese circled warily over the stubblefield to which they had been coming to feed for a week now. Reassured by the presence of half a dozen other pink-feet, which were already settled there, they glided down to land. Another skein followed, another and another, while the sky was filled with the clamour of thousands more geese. Before long, the original half-dozen, which had not stirred so much as a feather, were surrounded by a great multitude.

For those six placid birds were decoys and the whole strident gathering of the wild geese was being eagerly watched by two distinguished modern British ornithologists, Peter Scott and the late James Fisher,★ together with a team of helpers, in a wheeled hide at the edge of the field. Tensely they waited until the vast flock was feeding, hoping desperately that nothing would disturb the birds. Then, at a whispered signal, powerful rockets were set off; out they hissed, bearing immense catching-nets in a great arc.

With a roar of wings, the startled pink-feet took off, mounting urgently into the sky. But underneath the nets at least a hundred of them were trapped. Swiftly, expertly, the watchers hurried out to start the work of taking the struggling birds out of the nets. One by one they carried them to the ringer, who slipped a numbered and addressed metal ring on each bird's leg and closed the ring with pliers, after which the pink-foot was immediately released.

Such ringing operations are nowadays a highly organized matter and are of immense scientific value in studying the migration of birds, their numbers, their favourite feeding or nesting grounds, their length of life, and in many instances help to preserve endangered species. Besides, as Peter Scott has said, even though 'the study of birds only rarely has any significance in the field of economics, mankind would be the poorer without a capacity to be curious about the living creatures which share his world'.

Though he would have been astonished (but also struck with admiration) at the use of rockets for spreading the catching-nets over the wild geese, Charles Waterton – the Squire, as he was always known – would have appreciated the practice of ringing for the furtherance of ornithological studies. For Waterton (1782–1865) was certainly a pioneer in marking birds for

Using their newly invented rocket-nets in 1950–1, the Severn Wildfowl Trust's netting team caught and ringed nearly seven hundred pink-footed geese in Scotland for marking purposes. A similar method, using small cannons for propulsion, was tried out in America at about the same time. (Below) Peter Scott ringing a pink-footed goose.

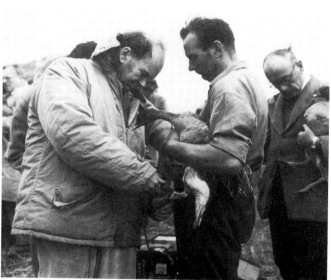

★Recounted in their book, *One Thousand Geese* (1953). The rocket nets were invented and developed by the Severn Wildfowl Trust in 1948.

Walton Hall, Charles Waterton's ancestral home. Great would have been his chagrin if he could have foreseen that after his death it would be bought up by the very soap manufacturer about whose objectionable activities nearby he had gone to law – unsuccessfully.

the purpose of identification. Evidently he had not heard of Frederick II 'ringing' a carp, and he would have been furious with envy to learn of Audubon's 'banding' attempts. (And how intrigued he would have been at the idea of a polar bear's movements being monitored over hundreds of miles of the Arctic by means of a miniature radio transmitter.) Ringing did not occur to Waterton: he simply clipped the tail of a bird so that he could subsequently pick it out individually.

Nevertheless, it was a highly advanced idea for the time and not the Squire's only one by any means. He also used decoy geese on the lake of Walton Hall, his ancestral home in Yorkshire, not for shooting purposes (as might have been expected of a contemporary of Colonel Peter Hawker, who regarded anything less than a dozen brace of a morning as much a misfortune as would have been the loss of his purse or watch), but in order to encourage visiting wildfowl. For smaller birds Waterton erected special nesting-boxes, some of them like modern observation-boxes in which, simply by moving a specially inserted stone, he could see the nest and its occupants.

As for sand-martins, in order to attract them to Walton where they had never nested before, he had a special bank built with holes in it for their use. Its success was instantaneous. The very next summer sand-martins nested there for the first time ever.

Nor did the Squire forget potential watchers, himself in particular. He built hides – 'substantial hovels', he called them – at favourable places where birds could be observed at leisure. So that inclement weather should not impede his bird-watching, he had a telescope set up in his drawing-room, from which he kept watch on his rookery and heronry.

Yet Waterton's greatest innovation was to turn the 259 acres of the Walton estate into a bird sanctuary, a truly remarkable idea for an age whose prim concept of nature could be summed up by Tennyson's

> Come into the garden, Maud,
>   For the black bat, night, has flown,
> Come into the garden, Maud,
>   I am here at the gate alone;
> And the woodbine spices are wafted abroad,
>   And the musk of the roses blown.

'The chief way to encourage birds is to forbid the use of firearms in the place of their resort. I have done so here; and to this precaution I chiefly owe my unparalleled success.' Waterton's head gamekeeper did not take kindly to the eccentric order that not even birds of prey should be killed. He was only persuaded otherwise when the Squire caught him in the act of shooting at some tawny owls. 'I threatened to strangle him if ever, after this, he molested either the old birds or their young ones.'

At great expense and financial sacrifice, Waterton threw a high wall round his entire estate, a project that took ten years. Because of a promise to one of his Jesuit masters at Stonyhurst College, Lancashire, he was a lifelong teetotaller and he reckoned he paid for the wall by the saving he made on the wines and spirits he would probably otherwise have bought.

The wall was intended to discourage foxes and badgers, but especially to keep out two-legged marauders. It does not seem to have succeeded in either case. In his *Autobiography* the Squire recounts with characteristic gusto a fearsome encounter with poachers who first of all

Waterton's portrait hangs in the National Portrait Gallery, London, and seems to belie the wilder aspects of his character. Waterton was buried on the shore of the lake, and his grave remains marked by the original cross. But the twin oaks that used to stand guard over him have long since fallen.

tried to knife him, then strangle him with his own cravat. But 'with one last convulsive effort, just as all was apparently over', he managed to put them to flight, leaving behind twenty snares. As for the four-legged visitors, they were tolerated, and Waterton, who could climb like a monkey and preferred to do so barefoot, used to take station at the top of an old oak-tree to keep watch on a fox-earth underneath.

Thus seated aloft, I could see the cubs as playful as kittens, catching each other by their brushes, now standing on three legs as if in the act of listening, then performing somersaults, sometimes snarling, sometimes barking, and often playing at a kind of hide-and-seek. On one occasion when I was keeping watch, old Reynard brought a fine pike, weighing, I should say, full three pounds, to the mouth of the hole, and instantly it was worried by the brood of cubs.

'Look here upon this picture, and on this.' This caricature of Waterton is in striking contrast to his portrait and sums up much of the spiteful contemporary view of him.

(Opposite above) The Aurochs, *Bos primigenius*, ancestor of our domestic cattle but extinct in Europe since the seventeenth century. From Gesner's *Historia animalium* (Zurich, 1551).

(Opposite below) A dromedary from the same edition. The Arabian camel, single-humped as distinct from the two-humped Bactrian, has been domesticated for nearly four thousand years.

The Squire continued climbing trees, partly for observation purposes, partly for sheer enjoyment, even in old age. For he was extremely athletic – and, one supposes, double-jointed. Dr Hobson, his physician and old friend, wrote: 'When Mr Waterton was seventy-seven years of age, I was witness to his scratching the back part of his head with the big toe of his right foot.' Waterton once climbed to the top of St Peter's in Rome and left his gloves on the lightning-conductor as a token of his visit.

The only creature Waterton would not tolerate was the rat, more precisely the brown rat – and more precisely still in his book, the 'Hanoverian' rat. The Watertons were devout Roman Catholics and fervent Stuart supporters. Waterton's father had been convinced that the brown rat had entered Britain not only at the same time as the detested usurpers, but in the very same ship that brought the Elector to his newly acquired throne.

Walton Park Hall was plagued by these 'Hanoverians' and Waterton waged total war against them. He used all manner of means to get rid of the rats. He let loose a fierce Demerara wild cat or 'marjay' which he had brought home from South America. He caught an old buck rat, dipped its hindquarters in tar and set it free in the hope of discouraging the others. He invented a special stone trap baited with 'an enticing and fatal powder made up of brown sugar, oatmeal and arsenic, all well triturated in a mortar'.

But he did not get rid of the rats.

He was a constant and devoted observer, for he knew that field-work was the only true way of learning the secrets of nature. He counted the number of times a pair of birds would visit their nest; observed the area from which they gathered their food. He timed barn owls bringing mice to their young; examined their pellets and proved how beneficial owls were in keeping down grain-eating pests. Likewise he came to realize that rogues though they might be in some ways, carrion crows and magpies also did good in eating noxious insects. 'Every bird, be his qualities "bad" or "good", is now welcome here, and still nothing seems to go wrong, either in the orchard or the garden.' For, far in advance of his time, he fully appreciated the balance of nature and the fact that predators had an essential part in fulfilling 'Nature's great plan'.

It was an abiding principle, passion almost, with Wat-

erton that everything, all knowledge, had to be acquired by personal observation. This occasionally led him obstinately to refute claims which are now well established, such as the fact that a young cuckoo will eject eggs from its foster home. His attitude came about simply because his nature demanded that he must see with his own keen eyes before he would believe. That principle is especially evident in his *Wanderings in South America* – Guiana, to be exact – for which he became famous and upon which he embarked towards the end of the Napoleonic Wars.

For instance, he wanted to test the alleged bloodsucking propensities of the vampire bat:

I had often wished to have been once sucked by the vampire in order that I might have it in my power to say it had really happened to me. There can be no pain in the operation, for the patient is always asleep when the Vampire is sucking him; and as for the loss of a few ounces of blood, that would be a trifle in the long run. Many a night have I slept with my foot out of the hammock to tempt the winged surgeon, expecting that he would be there, and I could never account for his not doing so, for we were inhabitants of the same loft for months together.

Deadly serious though he was, there is a faint air of comedy about the idea of the Squire diligently sticking his big toe out night after night in the interests of science. But he always had great faith in phlebotomy as a therapeutical exercise and Dr Hobson chided him for too often 'tapping his claret'.

Again, Waterton wanted to see how the poison of a snake was 'delivered' from its fangs. So he caught a labarri or fer de lance, one of the deadliest of snakes,

Not all Waterton's learned audience at the Scarborough meeting had confidence in his herpetological skill. Nearly 2,500 kinds of snake exist in the world, and of these some 250 are venomous to man. Two types of venom exist: a nerve poison secreted by cobras, for example, which causes paralysis of the respiratory muscles, and viper and rattlesnake venom, which is a blood poison.

whose poison is very fast-acting and was especially dangerous in days before anti-venine became available.

He was about eight feet long. I held him by the neck, and my hand was so near his jaw that he had not room to bite it. This was the only position I could have held him in with safety and effect. To do so it only required a little resolution and coolness. I then took a small piece of stick in the other hand and pressed it against the fang, which is invariably in the upper jaw. Towards the point of the fang there is a little oblong aperture on the convex side of it. Through this there is a little bag containing the poison. Now, when the point of the fang is pressed, the root of the fang also presses against the bag, and sends up a portion of the poison therein contained. Thus, when I applied a piece of stick to the point of the fang, there came out of the hole a liquor thick and yellow, like strong camomile tea. This was the poison which is so dreadful in its effect as to render the Labarri-snake one of the most poisonous in the forests of Guiana.

Waterton's famous ride on the cayman. The order of Crocodilia contains some twenty-five species, ranging from the formidable Nile crocodile, which has reached sixteen feet in length and claimed many human victims, to the five-foot long Chinese alligator of the Yangtze Kiang, which spends the winter snugly in the mud.

But the Squire was always cool-headed. At a scientific meeting he was addressing in Scarborough, Yorkshire, the learned audience began to stampede from the room when a demonstration rattlesnake escaped. But there was no need for panic. As Dr Hobson reports, 'Mr Waterton, who was as composed as if nothing particular had happened, promptly laid hold of the enraged reptile' and put it back in its box.

No doubt the best-known and most frequently repeated example of Waterton's 'do-it-yourself' approach to nature was his adventure with a black cayman, an alligator that can reach fifteen feet in length. He wanted a specimen for skinning and dissection, and, needless to say, he had to obtain one himself. For though the Indians brought him various examples, they were nearly always too damaged to be of any use to a naturalist. Eventually his men managed to trap a cayman on a cluster of large baited hooks. The Indians were horrified to learn that Waterton proposed that they should haul the animal out of the water alive. His Negro assistant, Daddy Quashy, suggested instead that it should be shot – whereupon the Squire threatened to knock him down for his cowardice (shades of his reaction to the gamekeeper!). So they duly dragged the cayman out on a rope. The plunging creature, however, was not easily subdued.

By this time the Cayman was within two yards of me. I saw he was in a state of fear and perturbation; and I instantly sprang up, and jumped on his back, turning half round as I vaulted, so that I gained my seat with my face in a right position. I immediately seized his forelegs, and, by main force, twisted them on his back; thus they served me for a bridle. He now seemed to have recovered from his surprise, and probably fancying himself in hostile company, he began to plunge furiously, and lashed the sand with his long and powerful tail. I was out of the reach of the strokes of it, by being near his head. He continued to plunge and strike, and made my seat very uncomfortable. It must have been a fine sight for an unoccupied spectator.

Well might Dr Hobson write: 'He knew no fear; and in daring enterprise, or in what is vulgarly termed "pluck", my friend signally excelled in comparison with the amount usually allotted to man.'

Leaving aside his South American 'Wanderings', Waterton led a strange and lonely existence. When he was forty-seven, he married the seventeen-year-old daughter of a friend he had made in Guiana, Anne Mary Edmondstone. She died the following year, three weeks after giving birth to a son. The Squire never recovered from his grief, and his loneliness and eccentricity only increased. He became even more ascetic in his ways, never slept again in a bed, simply wrapping himself in an Italian military cloak and using a block of wood for a pillow. He rose at three every morning, breakfasted on dry toast and milkless tea, dressed in workman's clothes, spent the first hours in prayer in the family chapel, then in reading Shakespeare or Dante or Horace.

Perhaps if he had had the calming influence of a wife throughout his life he would have made an even greater contribution to natural history. For as a naturalist he was undoubtedly a brilliant 'natural'. By his field-work he did much to dissipate the dry-as-dust atmosphere that pervaded the subject of natural history. Moreover, he exposed many errors that had been bandied about and brought to light many new facts. He showed, for example, that the ant-bear had two large glands from which 'is emitted a glutinous liquid with which his long tongue is lubricated when he puts it into the ants' nests'. He disproved the legend that the sloth was 'in a perpetual state of pain, that he is proverbially slow in his movements, and that, as soon as he has consumed all the leaves of the tree upon which he had mounted, he rolls himself up in the form of a ball and then falls to the ground'. If the 'closet' naturalists, as he mockingly termed them, *had gone into the wild* in order to examine the 'haunts and economy' of animals they purported to be acquainted with, they would not have gone on repeating their inaccurate conclusions. Waterton would have found much to admire in Frederick II, but he would not have approved of the Emperor's anti-papal activities.

The Squire was a born experimenter. One of his chief purposes in visiting the Brazilian border when he was in Guiana was to obtain samples of 'Wourali' (curare), a poison used by Indians to coat their arrowheads. He was convinced that wourali could be used as an antidote in hydrophobia or rabies. Back at home he had hopes of trying out his theory on a policeman in Nottingham who had been bitten by a rabid dog while on night

Waterton was an expert taxidermist, and he delighted in turning his skill to comic effect. Here, with the aid of a hedgehog, he has portrayed John Bull loaded down with the National Debt. An elephant might have been more appropriate.

patrol. Waterton hastened to the scene, but the unfortunate constable expired before he could get to work. After that the Squire had to be content with experimenting on donkeys. But he applied the dose too enthusiastically. The first donkey died on the spot. The second had to be revived by means of bellows being blown through her windpipe. In tribute, the Squire named her Wouralia, and she lived out the rest of her long life as a pensioner at Walton.

In spite of his brilliance Waterton was never really accepted by contemporary scientists. It should be mentioned here that because he was a Roman Catholic (and an extremely fervent one at that) he was debarred from many spheres of activity, for Catholic emancipation did not come about until 1829. His fellows held it against him that he had no scientific training; he would not even use Latin nomenclature – in spite of larding his writings with Latin tags from Ovid and Horace – and of course the naturalists could never, never forgive that 'closet' jibe. It was too near the truth for many of them. And then Waterton was often provocative. He pooh-poohed Darwin and his theories. The ape, he asserted, 'could lay no manner of claim to the most remote alliance with the human race, saving in faint appearance of form, and in nothing more', and to demonstrate his fair-mindedness in the matter, he took it upon himself, at the age of eighty, to sit in close embrace with a caged orang-utan. He waged a constant vendetta against Audubon, calling him a humbug and a charlatan on the basis of various discrepancies in the American's paintings. And without ever having set foot in Africa, he gave vent to some ludicrous statements about Paul du Chaillu – the subject of a later chapter. Worst of all, he was a practical joker, an unforgivable sin in a naturalist. (He would probably have enjoyed the Piltdown hoax.)

Waterton was an expert taxidermist and evolved a special method of preparing his specimens in corrosive sublimate dissolved in alcohol. Needless to say, most of his work in this field was of a serious nature and he had plenty of scope in all the many specimens he brought home from his four 'Wanderings' in South America. But he could not resist turning his skill to comic effect. In his otherwise admirable natural history museum at Walton Park was a section which he called 'England's Reformation Zoologically Illustrated'. This consisted of animal 'likenesses' of his Protestant *bêtes noires*. John Knox appeared as a black frog, while Luther was represented by a 'horrid incubus grinning and displaying the frightfully formidable tusks of a wild boar – the hands of a man – satanic horns – elephant's ears – bat's wings – one cloven foot, the other that of an eagle widely expanding his terrific-looking talons, and the tail of a serpent. . . .'

But the joke that caused most offence to the men of science was the Squire's celebrated Nondescript. He pretended that he had captured the creature in South America, but fearing to be overtaken by nightfall and not wishing to be burdened with the weight of a large animal, he contented himself with the head and shoulders which he brought back to Europe. In fact, the Nondescript was made from the skin of a red howler monkey which Waterton had manipulated with his usual skill so that it resembled a kind of simian gentleman of the

The Nondescript was Waterton's most notorious jape. But of course the Squire was not alone in mocking Darwin. *Punch* joined in the catcalls.

period. This Nondescript, he announced, was the missing link in the evolution of Man from an ape-like creature according to the theory recently advanced by Mr Charles Darwin.

Science was not amused. Probably the Nondescript did more harm to Waterton's reputation as a naturalist than anything else. This is an immeasurable pity, for the Squire deserves a far more prominent niche among the pioneers of natural history than he has received. As Richard Aldington has remarked, but for his frivolous side Waterton societies would flourish in Britain as surely as Audubon societies do in America.

Let Theodore Roosevelt have the last word: 'Waterton's *Wanderings* marked the beginning of the literature wherein field naturalists who are also men of letters have described for us the magic and interest, the terror and beauty of the far-off wilds where Nature gives peace to bold souls and inspires terror in the mind.'

9 Monuments to Nature

It might not altogether have pleased Charles Waterton to be found in such juxtaposition with Audubon as he is in this book. Nevertheless, in spite of the bitterness that existed between the 'charlatan' as Waterton dubbed Audubon and the 'Demarara gent.' as Audubon called the Squire, their intimate contact here is not inappropriate. For they were exact contemporaries; and while Waterton was virtually the first naturalist to venture into the wilds for his researches, for his part Audubon (with perhaps the earlier exception of that other American bird painter, Alexander Wilson) was the first artist to paint birds in their native haunts, to watch them mating, feeding, hunting, nesting, migrating. Throughout the ages mankind has wondered at and striven to emulate the sense of freedom envisioned in those wings of many colours. Only a man such as Audubon has captured some of their elusive beauty.

Audubon's father was a French merchant captain from Nantes, trading mainly in the Americas. Frequently he had to fight both for his life and his cargo – against the English. On the last occasion in 1779 he fought against overwhelming odds in the shape of four English 'corsairs', presumably privateers, as well as a couple of galleys, or so we are told – though the English were not in the habit of using galleys as were the French and Spanish. They sent convicts to the hulks or to Botany Bay, but not to man the sweeps.

Anyway, Captain Audubon was captured, together with his ship, the *Comte d'Artois*, and imprisoned in New York – his ship being subsequently burned, after its cargo of sugar had been seized. The captain later got his own back, for after having been released, he joined the French naval forces aiding the American rebels and had the satisfaction of witnessing the surrender of General Cornwallis at Yorktown.

All this gave rise to a fondness for America. The gallant captain resumed his profitable trading activities between France and the West Indies and amassed a fortune as merchant, planter, and especially as dealer in slaves (two thousand francs a head at a time when that currency was much 'heavier' than today), and during this time he purchased a farm called Mill Grove, in Pennsylvania. It was his ownership of this farm that led to the creation of what Baron Georges Cuvier, the Franco-Swiss zoologist, called 'the most magnificent monument

which has yet been raised to ornithology'; in other words, the paintings that have delighted the world ever since Audubon created them.

Audubon's mother was a Creole – a native of Santo Domingo but of European descent. When she died, Captain Audubon returned to Nantes with Jean-Jacques (also known, perhaps appropriately, as Fougère or Fern) and his sister, who were generously accepted by the captain's lawful wife. Her attitude was later summed up by Audubon the artist thus: 'Let no one speak of her as my stepmother. I was ever to her as a son of her own flesh and blood, and she was to me a true mother.'

She also boasted that Jean-Jacques was the handsomest boy in France, which must have gratified him, for he was always conscious of his good looks and once wrote:

It was fortunate for posterity that Audubon's father bought the farm at Mill Grove (pictured here). For the idea of John James becoming manager of it was the cause of Audubon's settling in America, his latent genius being sparked off by the riches of nature he found there.

I measured five feet ten and a half inches, was of fair mien, and quite a handsome figure; large, dark, and rather sunken eyes, light-coloured eyebrows, aquiline nose and a fine set of teeth; hair, fine texture and luxuriant, divided and passing down behind each ear in luxuriant ringlets as far as the shoulders.

A fine figure of a man to stride the American wilds; but not necessarily complacent – he was probably looking at himself with the analytical eye of a portraitist, which he was before birds came to absorb him utterly.

Lucy Bakewell

(Opposite) 'In person he was tall and slender,' wrote a woman contemporary of Audubon, 'his blue eyes were an eagle's in brightness. He was very sociable and communicative, being the centre of attraction in every circle in which he mingled. Audubon was abstemious in his diet and did not drink tea nor coffee nor did he use tobacco. He always drank a glass of weak whisky and water, which he called grog, for his breakfast.'

Captain Audubon brought his children to France soon after the outbreak of the French Revolution. When Jean-Jacques was about eight, the Terror of 1793 flared up. So it is not surprising that his formal education was to all intents and purposes non-existent, from which posterity profited. For he spent most of his time ranging along the idyllic banks of the Loire. Before long pencil and crayon came into his hands and his course was set.

It seems that a debt is owed by posterity to the young Audubon's indulgent stepmother. Captain Audubon

fondly hoped that his son would become an engineer or at least follow him to sea. But the captain was away too often to keep an eye on Jean-Jacques, who, with the tacit connivance of Madame Audubon, dodged school whenever he could and took to that other 'school' from which he benefited far more. His lessons may have been neglected but he could in truth have said, 'In nature's infinite book of secrecy/A little can I read'. As far as his drawing is concerned, his main training seems to have been a brief spell in the studio of J.L. David, known principally for his *Portrait of Madame Récamier*. Nothing could be in greater contrast with that elegant drawing-room piece than the wild freshness that Audubon was to capture.

The reasons for Audubon's returning to America could have been threefold. Perhaps Captain Audubon gave up the unequal struggle as far as his son's education was concerned. Perhaps he dreaded the thought of the young man being swallowed up in the maw of conscription, ever more voracious because of the demands of Napoleon. Perhaps he was concerned about his property in Pennsylvania. Almost as soon as he had purchased Mill Grove, with its 285 acres of farm and woodland and mineral rights, he had leased out the property. By 1803 that lease had come to an end, so, hoping that Jean-Jacques would prove an efficient manager of it, Captain Audubon packed his son off across the Atlantic, with all its attendant wartime hazards. Those hazards were very real and when Audubon, after a brief visit to see his parents, was returning in 1806 to America, the United States ship in which he was a passenger, the *Polly,* was boarded en route by H.M.S. *Rattlesnake*. Fortunately Audubon's passport stated that he had been born in New Orleans, otherwise he might have ended up in the prisoner-of-war camp on Dartmoor in Devon, where so many French prisoners languished – to be joined in 1812 by American sailors.

Audubon's initial arrival in what was to become his adopted country was not auspicious. He promptly went down with yellow fever, from which he would probably have died but for the care taken of him by two Quaker women in New Jersey. As for Mill Grove, not only was John James (as we must now call him) never interested in mineral rights or livestock or milling, but he entered into some unfortunate partnerships and business transactions

In *Les Mohicans de Paris* Alexander Dumas wrote: 'There is a woman in every case; as soon as they bring me a report, I say, "Look for the woman".' The woman in Audubon's case was Lucy Bakewell (depicted on previous page), daughter of an emigrant English farmer. Without her unflagging support, in all their tribulations and shifting from pillar to post, Audubon's great life-work would never have materialized. As this illustration of one of the Audubon's homes shows, the houses the Americans built in those days reflected the sense of spaciousness they enjoyed – and the notion that their forests were inexhaustible.

that were to bedevil him for a long time, and even bankrupt him.

However, to balance that and more, he always seems to have been lucky in his womenfolk: first with his kindly stepmother, and now, in spite of the bitterness of war, with an English wife. For when he was twenty-three he married Lucy Bakewell, daughter of an Englishman who had gone out to America in 1802 to take possession of the neighbouring 'Fatland Ford', as it was called. If posterity owes a debt to Audubon's stepmother for nurturing his passion for nature, it is even more in the debt of Lucy Bakewell. It was she who sustained him through all the hardships and setbacks that followed, she who encouraged him in his work, she who as governess or schoolmistress scraped together the money to support and educate their children, so that Audubon could be free to carry out his life's work in the American wilderness.

In the words of Francis Hobart Herrick, the generous, emotional, self-indulgent Audubon could have accomplished nothing but for the intelligent devotion of his capable wife. 'Without her zeal and self-sacrifice the world would never have heard of Audubon. His budding talents eventually would have been smothered in some backwoods town of the Middle West or South.'⋆

As well as becoming enamoured of Lucy Bakewell, Audubon fell in love with America. Wordsworth was writing about the French Revolution when he rhapsodized

> Bliss was it in that dawn to be alive,
> But to be young was very heaven!

but if by chance Audubon had come across those lines, well might he have linked them with his journeys down the Ohio and the Mississippi or through the creeks of Florida. His far wanderings originated partly through his business enterprises − lead-mine, sawmill, grist-mill, steamboat and so on. But his efforts at trading failed not simply as a result of the partnerships he naïvely entered into, but because his heart was elsewhere. The more he saw of nature, the more he became enraptured by it. He plunged, metaphorically and physically, deeper and deeper into the wilds.

One of his first ornithological activities was concerned with the western wood pewee, a delightful little flycatching bird. Not only were the pewees Audubon's first serious study of American birdlife, but also he 'banded' some of the young for identification purposes − what in Britain is called ringing. 'I fixed a light silver thread on the leg of each, loose enough not to hurt it, but so fastened that no exertion of theirs could remove it.' The numerous bird banding societies of America are the result of that enterprise.

Most bird paintings before Audubon's time had been done from stuffed specimens. This Audubon disliked, feeling rightly that the results were too stilted. He quickly evolved his own particular method, when he was studying the pewees. By the use of wires, with which wings or head or body or tail could be pierced, he would set up his model in whatsoever pose he desired, instead of being stuck with one single stereotyped example provided by the taxidermist. When a bird had been suitably arranged in an action pose, as it were, it was set against squared paper which matched the squares in which his drawing paper was divided. The fact, too, that he invariably drew his specimens life-size was an additional help in obtaining accuracy, for he measured every feature meticulously.

His 'method' inevitably demanded a vast number of specimens, and these he obtained himself by shooting. The portraits of him by George Healey, and by Audubon's sons John Woodhouse and Victor, show him with gun in arm.

At sunrise next morning, I and four negro servants proceeded in search of birds and adventures. The fact is that I was anxious to kill some twenty-five Brown Pelicans. I shot some rare birds, then putting along the shore, passed a point when, lo, I came in sight of several hundred pelicans, perched on the branches of mangrove trees, seated in comfortable harmony, as near each other as the strength of the branches would allow. I ordered to back water gently; the hands backed water. I waded to the shore under cover of the rushes along it, saw the pelicans fast asleep, examined their countenances and deportment well and leisurely, then levelled my firing-piece, fired and dropped two of the finest specimens I ever saw. I really believe I would have shot one hundred of these reverend sirs, had not a mistake taken place in the reloading of my gun. A mistake, however, did take place, and to my utmost disappointment, I saw each pelican, old and young, leave his perch, and take wing, soaring off, well pleased, I dare say, at making so good an escape from so dangerous a foe.

As Audubon put it, 'I shot, I drew, I looked on nature only. . . .' Both those other later painters of wildlife, J.G. Millais and Archibald Thorburn, were well known as shooting men.

Such was the wealth of birdlife at that time, when certain parts of the American landscape must have resembled some rich painting by Henri Rousseau, that Audubon, concerned only with his work, could have had no inkling of how swiftly the gun and other factors would change the face of nature in his adopted land, that the breath-taking flocks of passenger pigeons would vanish from the skies and that the bald eagle, America's

⋆Francis Hobart Herrick, *Audubon the Naturalist: A History of His Life and Time* (1938).

The American 'robin'
is a thrush, *Turdus
migratorius*. It breeds
from Alaska and
Newfoundland to
Mexico and Georgia.
It winters from
British Columbia and
Massachusetts to
Central America. In
character rather like a
blackbird, it is an
occasional
transatlantic passerine
vagrant.

Coccyzus americanus, the yellow-billed cuckoo, breeds from British Columbia and New Brunswick in the north to Mexico and the Florida Keys. Though Audubon shows it snatching a butterfly, its favourite food is hairy caterpillars.

national emblem, would become a rare bird. When in later years he travelled up the Missouri River in search of material for his *Quadrupeds of North America* he was horrified by the wholesale slaughter of the bison and wrote that 'before many years the Buffalo, like the Great Auk, will have disappeared'.

Though subsequent generations have reaped the benefit of Audubon's strenuous wanderings through North America, he and his family were a long time deriving any gain. He and his wife faced many adversities, too numerous to recount here. Sometimes, however, it was a case of the ill wind that brings good in its train. There came a time when John James was forced to take the post of tutor, at $60 a month, to instruct in dancing, drawing, mathematics, French and music (he was a fair violinist) Eliza Pirrie, daughter of a rich cotton planter at Feliciana in the state of Louisiana. We have already seen several instances of enlightened patronage – and America certainly has never lacked in this respect. Audubon was indeed fortunate in this encounter with the Pirrie family, for it was during his stay at Feliciana that he did some of his best and most famous work. The lovely blossoms of the magnolia woods were complemented by the brilliant colours of the birds that flashed by on every side. Mocking-birds, ivory-billed woodpeckers, golden orioles, roseate spoonbills – their beautiful hues inspired him almost feverishly. One of the paintings he did at Feliciana was the famous *Mocking-bird Defending Its Nest against a Rattlesnake*. It was this 'notorious reptile' to which Waterton so fiercely reacted later on in his running fight with Audubon (egged on by George Ord, champion of the less well known Alexander Wilson).

Finished drawing a very fine specimen of a rattle-snake, which measured five feet and seven inches, weighed six and a quarter pounds and had seven rattles. Anxious to give it a position most interesting to a naturalist, I put it in that which the reptile commonly takes when on the point of striking madly with its fangs. I had examined many before, and especially the position of the fangs along the superior jawbones, but had never seen one showing the whole of its fangs exposed at the same time.

Or shaped like that! thundered the Squire. For Waterton, jealous of his reputation as a herpetologist, described Audubon's representation as 'nothing but a fabulous Hydra, with its eyes starting out of their sockets' and its fangs drawn in a totally inaccurate fashion. This was not by any means the only occasion on which the Yorkshireman and the French-American clashed. Apart from the descriptions in Wilson's *American Ornithology* and the classification of Linnaeus, Audubon had little reference material to help him. So in the mass of work which he did it was inevitable that he should make some mistakes, for example in sometimes claiming to identify a new species when it was actually the young of a bird already known. A case in point is that of the bald eagle, which Waterton seized on, quite justifiably as it happened. Another famous controversy was over whether the vulture located its prey by scent or by sight. In his *Wanderings*, Waterton had more than once emphatically declared that it was the vulture's olfactory sense that mattered: 'When the scent of carrion has drawn together hundreds of vultures.' As in the case of ringing the carp,

Waterton does not seem to have heard of Frederick II's experiments on the subject; nor for that matter had Audubon. But Audubon reached the same conclusion as the Emperor – namely, that vultures do find their prey by sight. This was borne out by Audubon's friend, the Reverend John Bachman who, angered by such attacks on the painter, described a number of experiments he and John James had carried out with the life-size painting of a sheep skinned, cut open and placed in the open. 'No sooner was this picture placed on the ground than the Vultures observed it, alighted nearby, walked over to it, and commenced tugging at the painting.'

All this is of course anticipating events, for the feud (mainly conducted by the Squire) did not arise until some years later. Meanwhile, Audubon was obliged to quit his pleasant haven at Feliciana somewhat abruptly. This was possibly owing to jealousy on the part of the family doctor who was enamoured of the Miss Pirrie. After all, Audubon was undoubtedly a handsome and dashing figure. It was not surprising that a legend of his being the lost Dauphin had gone the rounds.

Troubles come not single spies, for as soon as he left the Pirrie ménage, Audubon was downcast to find that some two hundred of his drawings had been ruined through a gunpowder flask leaking in the chest they were kept in. But that was nothing compared with an earlier calamity when rats reared a family in another chest. They proceeded to gnaw their way through paintings of 'nearly a thousand inhabitants of the air'.

However, Audubon, sustained by Lucy, recovered from each of these setbacks and went to work more actively than ever. By 1826 he had enough drawings for his *Birds of America*, the four volumes of which, augmented by work done on subsequent expeditions to Labrador and the Great Plains, were published in England between 1827 and 1838. The friends he made in Britain ranged from Sir Walter Scott to the Tyneside engraver Thomas Bewick, and his success was as wide-ranging as his friendships when his pictures were exhibited at the Royal Institution of Edinburgh. The French critic Philarète-Chasles spoke for many when he wrote:

A magic power transported us into the forests which for so many years this man of genius has trod. The plumage of the birds sparkle with nature's own tints;

vespertilio Audubonii —

To Richard Harlan Esqre M.D.
&c &c &c
with the good wishes of his Oblig'd friend
John J. Audubon
Camden Sep 25 1829.

you see them in motion or at rest, in their play and in their combat, in their anger and their affection, singing, running, asleep, just awakened, beating the air, skimming the waves, or rending one another in their battles. It is a real and palpable vision of the New World, with its atmosphere, its imposing vegetation, and its tribes which know not the yoke of man. The sun shines athwart the clearing in the woods; the swan floats suspended between a cloudless sky and a glittering wave; strange and majestic figures keep pace with the sun, which gleams from the mica sown broadcast on the shores of the Atlantic; and this realization of an entire hemisphere, this picture of a nature so lusty and strong, is owing to the brush of a single man; such an unheard of triumph of patience and genius! – the resultant rather of a thousand triumphs won in the face of innumerable obstacles.

The Chiroptera (meaning 'hand-winged') are the order of bats, the only mammals that can truly fly. They range from the so-called flying fox or Malayan fruit bat, with a wing-span of almost five feet, to the tiny pipistrelle with a spread of eight inches. Not forgetting the Squire's old bed-mate, the vampire bat. But even the real great blood-sucking bat does not *suck* its victim's blood. With razor-sharp teeth it makes an incision in the hide of sleeping cow or horse and *laps* the blood with its long tongue.

During his visit to Australia, John Gould was fascinated by kangaroos – not surprisingly, as the species only became known through Captain Cook and Banks. Gould devoted the whole of Volume 2 of his *Mammals of Australia* to the kangaroo family.

Nowadays, first editions of those four volumes, comprising 435 plates, can fetch more than £200,000 a set. Such a figure is perhaps reflective of the pleasure and delight that Audubon's paintings have given to successive generations.

The glamour surrounding Audubon has always tended to overshadow his younger contemporary, John Gould. This was partly because of the romance of the American wilderness with which John James had become identified, and partly because Gould was far more of a museum painter, as it was termed, and spent infinitely less time in the wild. Gould was born at Lyme in Dorset in 1804, the year after Audubon set sail for America. His first job as a boy was helping his father, who was a gardener in the Royal Gardens at Windsor. Then as a young man he became gardener at Ripley Castle in Yorkshire. But unlike his other contemporary, David Douglas, it was not to botany that he was drawn. It was the colours of the birds in the garden that touched his imagination rather than the flowers.

Audubon went to America, Gould to London; and that perhaps sums up the difference between the two men. Be that as it may, this prosaic move was a turning-point for the latter. In 1827, thanks to N.A. Vigors, an ex-Guards officer, future Member of Parliament, a capable amateur naturalist, and first secretary of the newly established Zoological Society, Gould was appointed 'naturalist' to that august body.

Audubon got his inspiration direct from nature. True, as has been said, he shot wholesale to obtain his models, but at the same time he was able to study them in their natural surroundings. Gould's inspiration came to him otherwise. In 1830 the Zoological Society acquired a large collection of stuffed birds from the Himalayas, including many hitherto unknown to European naturalists. It was on this collection of the taxidermist's skill that Gould proposed to base his first book. Vigors gave him every encouragement and took it upon himself to write the text (when Audubon compiled his *Ornithological Biographies* he had employed William MacGillivray, author of *British Birds*, to write the scientific descriptions).

Gould was fortunate in another respect, too. If Lucy Bakewell had given Audubon moral support, Gould's wife was not only his faithful companion but his work-

mate as well; any credit given to John Gould should be shared with her. For while Gould did the original drawings (which some people considered more vigorous than the finished articles), she it was who made the final drawings and transposed them to the plates. Thanks to a German invention at the end of the eighteenth century, lithography was now in practical use and was rapidly superseding copper-plate engraving. In Britain Rudolph Ackermann had first used the process in 1812 for his *Series of Thirty Studies from Nature*, and the geologist William Smith included lithographic illustrations in his *Strata Identified by Organized Fossils*. Immediately before Gould came on the scene, William Swainson had used lithography for his *Zoological Illustrations*. By the time Gould had need of it, the technique of lithography had greatly improved and he seized joyfully on it as a means

Portrait of a Say's squirrel, one of Audubon's quadrupeds. Members of the Rodentia, squirrels are well adapted for life in the trees, their long bushy tails acting as rudders in their vaulting activities. The so-called flying squirrels cannot actually fly: flaps of skin joining their limbs enable them to glide upwards of sixty yards from tree to tree.

Audubon's smew, *Mergellus albellus*, the smallest of the mergansers, is a native of northern Europe and Asia. In winter it visits the Atlantic and Mediterranean coasts and some European lakes.

(Opposite) William Vogt described Cuvier's regulus (named in honour of the French anatomist) as 'another of Audubon's unknown birds', and the American Ornithological Union Check-list noted that no similar bird had ever been seen. 'Audubon's memory has been proved faulty on more than one point, but in this failing he is not unique. Naturalists – including amateurs – do well to take careful notes on the spot!'

Cuvier's Wren
Regulus Cuvierii
Kalmia Latifolia

of reproducing both his skill and the colours and detail of nature in a way that had not been possible before.

Even so, Gould, like Audubon, had the utmost difficulty in even getting a publisher to look at his work because of the enormous expense that would be involved in bringing out the kind of book he planned. Not to be cheated of the success he was confident in, Gould became his own publisher. His confidence was amply justified, for his *One Hundred Birds of the Himalayas* had a *succès fou*. Perhaps because he had a good, highly respectable position and also because he realized there was among the growing band of amateur natural history enthusiasts an expanding market for his work anyway, Gould was not interested in plunging headlong into nature as Audubon had done. He drew largely on museums at home and abroad for his material, supplementing this by widespread acquaintance with naturalists, which was not very difficult in view of his links with Regent's Park in London.

All this was the basis for his *Birds of Europe* which appeared between 1832 and 1837 and comprised about 450 plates. However, when he started work on his *Birds of Australia* he came to the conclusion, not surprisingly, that he was in urgent need of first-hand material. There-

fore, always supremely energetic and enterprising, he promptly decided to go to Australia. His wife went with him and did a great deal of work for him, not only on birds but also on flowers for the background of the plates; rather as Joseph Mason had done for Audubon, though neither Mrs Gould nor Mason seems to have received just credit.

Soon after they returned from that far journey in 1840, Gould's wife died. The effect this event must have had on him is evidenced by the fact that publication of *Birds of Australia* was not achieved until 1848. However, when Gould had recovered from this heartfelt blow, his energy returned. *Birds of Australia* was followed, in 1849, by a monograph on humming-birds, which revealed that his enterprise had not diminished. Having finished with the humming-birds as subjects for his illustrations, he exhibited his collection in a specially constructed building at the Zoological Society in order to take advantage of the crowds flocking to the Great Exhibition of 1851. Gould's 'Trochilidae' proved to be one of the biggest draws of all – and a very profitable one for him.

Like Audubon, who had painted grizzly bears, moose, buffaloes and wolves, Gould too turned his hand to mammals. He produced a monograph on kangaroos and a three-volume work on the mammals of Australia. But his first and greatest enthusiasm was always birds, and his *Birds of Great Britain*, a five-volume work he embarked on in 1873, was his most popular and crowning success.

Artists in any medium, generally speaking, are not well versed in worldly matters. Gould, however, never despised any monetary reward that came his way; nor did he suffer the poverty that so often beset Audubon. He made large sums from his work (a pleasant change from the frequent instances of some speculator profiting after an artist's death) and he knew how to drive a bargain. On his return from Australia he offered his large collection of skins and eggs and mounted specimens to the British Museum for £1,000. Alternatively, he said, the museum could have the collection free if it subscribed for twenty-five copies of his coming work on Australia. The authorities declined the offer and the collection ended up in the Academy of Natural Sciences in Philadelphia.

Gould is said to have left £80,000, and as Dr Herrick has remarked, he was perhaps the only ornithologist who ever grew rich in his profession.

10 'Man of Grass'

'When he has learnt that bottiney means a knowledge of plants, he goes and knows 'em. That's our system, Nickleby; what so you think of it?' Thus Mr Squeers, and the facetious words of Dickens sum up the attitude of many people to botany. It has so often been looked upon as faintly ludicrous, a pastime for parsons and genteel ladies. But let alone the antarctic adventures of a plant-hunter such as Joseph Hooker, or Frank Kingdon-Ward scrambling in the Himalayas, or even Linnaeus's uncomfortable perambulations in Lapland, there could be no greater refutation of the attitude than the brief career of David Douglas.

No doubt his tough childhood helped him in what was to come, for Douglas did indeed need every ounce of that toughness, physical and moral. Not only did he come from a poor family – his father being grandly termed a stonemason, though in reality he seems to have been an odd-job man – but he was the black sheep of the village school at Scone in Perthshire. He was sent to school at the highly unusual age of three by a mother anxious to get him out of the way of his bad-tempered father whom he closely resembled; a fact which led to constant feuding between them. Even the 'tawse' enthusiastically applied by successive masters had no effect – or rather, an even more adverse effect. David simply played truant to an increasing extent until, a veteran of ten, he was flung out of school for the last time.

Though, as is evident, his blackavised father wove no flowers about his cradle, they were nevertheless the same inspiration for David Douglas as they had been for Linnaeus, undoubtedly a result of his lonely wanderings while he was playing hookey. After all the turmoil of his childhood his fortunes took a turn for the better. A friend of the Douglas family, William Beattie, head gardener to the Earl of Mansfield at the Old Palace of Scone, ancient coronation site of Scottish kings, offered David a job. Thanks partly to the encouragement of George III and his mother Queen Augusta, Kew Gardens had already been established in 1760 and the aristocracy were increasingly beautifying their own properties in imitation.

It all worked like magic on this hitherto unruly limb of the de'il. After seven years' apprenticeship at Scone, he moved on to another fashionable garden, Valleyfield, near Culross, Fife, property of Sir Robert Preston, Baronet, a collector of orchids and other exotic plants. But

Portrait of David Douglas (artist unknown). The end of the Anglo-American War of 1812–14 marked another turning-point in American history. The young nation was beginning to realize the immensity of the land to the west – and into that virtually unknown land Douglas ventured.

the turning-point really came when he was taken on at the Glasgow Botanic Gardens, where he made a giant stride towards his ambition of becoming a botanist rather than merely a gardener.

Not only was the job itself a splendid opportunity for this now fanatical botanizer; more important, it brought him to the notice of Dr William Jackson Hooker, Professor of Botany at Glasgow University. Hooker later became Director of Kew Gardens, as did his equally illustrious son, Sir Joseph Dalton Hooker, friend of Darwin. To begin with, Hooker, later knighted, employed Douglas as his assistant on botanical tours in the Western Highlands, collecting material for his *Flora Scotica*, but very soon the professor and the young man were firm friends. In the second of his American expeditions, Douglas named one of the highest of the Rocky Mountains, a peak which he climbed without the aid of so

much as a walking-stick, in honour of 'the enlightened and learned Professor of Botany' to whose kindness he owed his success.

Hooker was so impressed with Douglas's talents that he recommended him to the Royal Horticultural Society as exactly the man they were looking for to go on a botanical expedition to North America. Douglas records that he set off on his first expedition in 1823 when he was completing his twenty-fourth year. Linnaeus had been twenty-five when he started his Lapland journey. Though plants in general were Douglas's brief, his first priority was to fetch specimens of American fruit trees. The voyage out from Liverpool took more than eight weeks and must have been uncomfortable and tedious to a degree. Fresh water had to be rationed, and when it rained the passengers took the opportunity of doing their laundry, their dogs licking the rain-swept decks. Afterwards the temperature reached ninety-six degrees Fahrenheit. A valuable horse died and its owner set the ship in an uproar because of his distress. Food began to run short, for many of the passengers 'found' for themselves. Nearly everyone was seasick, though not Douglas. He passed the time by reading his Spanish grammar (one of his later expeditions took him to hispanic California) and studying *Linnean Transactions*. He shot several sea-birds, intending them for specimens, but could not retrieve them because of the rough sea. He was frustrated in his wish to visit the Azores because of an outbreak there of smallpox, and had to content himself with a glimpse of plant life on the islands through the captain's spyglass.

Compared with his subsequent expeditions, Douglas's first visit to America was positively sedate.

I made a point of calling on W. Coxe Esq., who used me very hospitably. I saw his vast and extensive orchards. His trees are all in fine health, and he was just on the eve of commencing his cider harvest; he has in his garden a choice selection of peaches, apples, pears and so on. He gave me to understand that he would send the Society a collection of keeping fruit in the fall, after checking off what he considered to be new. . . .

. . . Called on Stephen van Ransaleer Esq., who is the most wealthy man in the United States. He has a large garden and orchards, and a fine range of hothouses,

(Left) Sir William Jackson Hooker. For many generations the Hooker family had lived in Exeter, but William was born in Norwich, in 1785. When he was twenty-four he made a botanical tour of Iceland, but his collection was destroyed by fire on board his ship – like Wallace's in South America a generation later. On another occasion the botanizing Hooker was bitten by a viper, did nothing about it, and suffered a long illness as a result.

(Below) A plan of the Botanic Garden at Glasgow where David Douglas first came in contact with Hooker. According to Joseph Dalton Hooker, his father was a 'vigorous pedestrian, covering sixty miles a day with ease'. Every Sunday he would walk twenty-two miles from his home in Helensburgh in order to be present at his eight o'clock lectures on Monday.

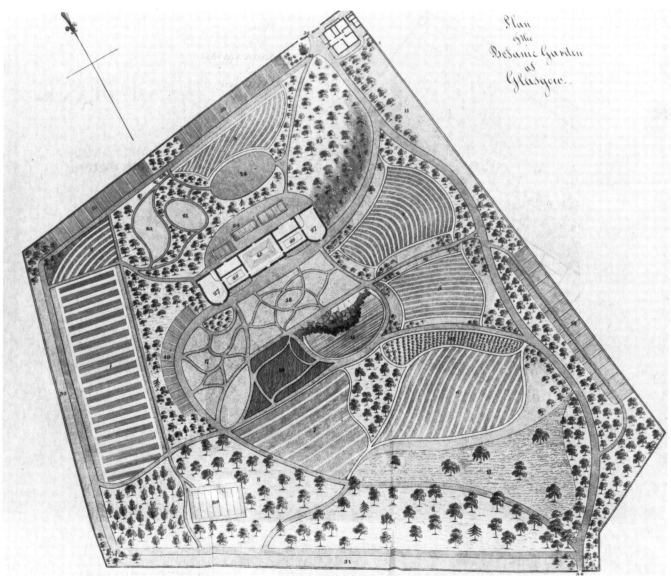

chiefly filled with vines. The grapes were all cut and hung on strings in a fruit-room. . . .

. . . I saw in Mr Thomson's garden peaches in particular in great vigour and health, neither pruned nor get any manure. . . .

His only adventure on this trip was on Lake Erie when 'we experienced a motion that could not be surpassed in an ocean. It blew a tempest the whole of the time. Towards midnight on Sunday we reached Buffalo, one of the wheels of the paddle-boat having been swept away, and otherwise disabled'. We have a nice hint of his earnest preoccupation with his mission. On arriving at Albany, he found the town *en fête* in celebration of the opening of the Western Canal, with guns firing, bands playing and general junketing. Not for David Douglas any such revelry. When at last he succeeded in finding a hotel room, he records: 'I unpacked my seeds, arranged, and put in fresh papers.'

Though Douglas's first visit to America was highly successful and provides a picture of some of the pleasant living that had been established on the East Coast, it was in total contrast with his next assignment. This took him to 'The North-Western parts of the Continent of North America' whither, in 1824, he sailed by way of Cape Horn in the *William and Ann*. En route, with the aid of the ship's surgeon John Scouler, an acquaintance from Glasgow days, he was active at any opportunity, making, among other things, a fine collection of orchids in Brazil. It is significant that the Royal Horticultural Society awarded the ship's captain their silver medal!

Douglas's real testing-time was to come and this expedition left its mark on him for the rest of his brief life. To put his achievements into perspective, it must be remembered that he had already been at school several years when Lewis and Clark had proved that the Pacific coast of America could be reached overland instead of by the long sea voyage round Cape Horn. Further, it was only fourteen years since Captain Robert Stuart had made the first west to east journey across America, and some of the conditions he described still obtained when David Douglas set forth.

As we were preparing for bed one night, after yet another near-starvation day, one of our men advanced towards me with his rifle in hand, saying that as there was no appearance of our being able to procure any provisions at least until we got to the extreme of this plain, which would take us three or four days, he was determined to go no farther, but that lots should be cast and one die to preserve the rest, adding as a farther inducement for me to agree to his proposal that I should be exempted in consequence of being their leader.

Acer macrophyllum. Hooker drew many of the specimens Douglas brought back.

Method and devotion are evident on every page of Douglas's journals. His brief life was an uninterrupted adventure story and it is strange that he remains so little known to most people.

I shuddered at the idea and used every endeavour to create an abhorrence in his mind against such an act, urging also the probability of our falling in with some animal on the morrow. But, finding that every argument failed and that he was on the point of converting some others to his cannibalistic purpose, I snatched up my rifle, cocked and levelled it at him with the firm resolution to fire if he persisted. This affair so terrified him that he fell instantly upon his knees and asked the whole party's pardon, solemnly swearing he should never again suggest such a thought.

After this matter was settled I felt so agitated and weak that I could scarcely crawl to bed.*

*Stuart became interested in the Far West through association with John Jacob Astor of fur-trade fame.

Though David Douglas was never forced to contemplate cannibalism − in any case he was more often than not on his own − he was often reduced to comparable circumstances. At least twice he had to slaughter one of his horses to save himself from starvation. Frequently there was nothing to eat but plants such as the arrowroot and wild liquorice Lewis and Clark had mentioned (much of the time he was in 'their' country). On one occasion, especially galling, he was reduced to eating the very specimens he had taken such pains to collect − a member of his party suffering 'some slight inconvenience' as a result. A quite typical extract from his *Journal* illustrates the hardships he endured in the cause of botany:

I was very hungry in the evening and went out and gathered a few bear-berries, being the only thing which could be found at the place. After the violent hurricane the wind was still so high, with heavy rain, that scarcely any fire could be made. Long ere day I was ready to leave Cape Foulweather, which name it merits; being in a very bad state for walking. All the wildfowl had fled to more sheltered parts; not a bird of any description could be seen. Being these two days without food, I resolved to endeavour to walk over the portage to the north side of Whitbey Harbour, where I was informed by my guide he expected a fishing-party from his village to be. On my arriving there at six o'clock in the evening, being on my legs from four in the morning, I can hardly give an idea of my afflicted state. The storm continued with equal violence, which prevented the fishing-party from leaving their village and thus increased my misery. While my Indians were collecting fuel, I made a small booth of pine branches, grass, and a few old mats; my blanket being drenched in wet the preceding day, and no opportunity of drying it, the night raining heavily, I deemed it prudent not to lie down to sleep. Therefore I spent this night at the fire. On Saturday I found myself so much broken down and my (festering) knee so much worse that I did not stir out for the whole of the day. A little before dusk the weather moderated, when I crawled out with my gun; providentially I killed five ducks with one shot, which, as might be expected, were soon cooked, though one of the In-

dians ate a part raw, the other did not bother to pluck the feathers off but literally burned them to save time.

At times he was so tired, not to mention that his deerskin shoes were insufficient protection for his feet, his knee was worse and his arthritis troubling him, that even when food was not difficult to come by, he was cheated of it.

I killed two partridges an hour before I camped, which I placed in my little kettle to boil for supper. The Canadians and my two Indians had eaten their dry salmon and were asleep. Before my birds were cooked Morpheus seized me also; I awoke at daybreak and beheld my supper burned to ashes and three holes in the bottom of my kettle.

On another hungry occasion when the company he was with (he often fell in with fur-trappers and traders) shot a Franklin's grouse, he would not allow it to be eaten, being anxious to preserve it for his scientific purposes.

Tea was always a sovereign remedy − the 'monarch' of all sustenance, as he called it. Sometimes the food it washed down was obtained by unorthodox means. Near Fort Vancouver Douglas records watching a silver-headed eagle take a sturgeon from the river, whereupon he promptly shot the bird. Its claws were so firmly embedded in the fish that he had to thrust a needle into the vertebrae of the bird's neck to disengage the mechanism. At times sturgeon were plentiful:

Our supper was a piece of good sturgeon, a basin of tea, and a slice of bread. I had six Indians for paddling the canoe; they sat round the fire the whole night roasting the sturgeon, which they do by splitting a branch and placing the meat on it, twisting a bit of rush at the top to prevent it falling out. They ate a fish weighing about twenty-eight pounds from ten o'clock at night till daylight. We had paddled forty miles without any sort of food except some wild shoots and water.

In the midst of all his hardships, he appreciated to the full the relief of a friendly welcome and a good bellyful of food, and speaks of the gratitude he felt when 'one caused water to be brought me to wash, while another was handing me a clean shirt and a third employing himself cooking my supper'. He remembers nostalgically an occasion near Edmonton when, after a 'walk' of forty-three miles through wretched country without a bite to eat, he suddenly heard the sweet music of sledge-dogs howling as night came on and caught sight of the fires of lodges, where he was regaled with fine moose-steaks. But such being the age, he was so conscious of his unkempt appearance that before arriving there he went back half a mile to a lake, stripped and plunged in, then put on a clean shirt. Perhaps that was the occasion when one of his new friends 'was called on to indulge us with a tune on the violin, to which he readily complied. No time was lost in forming a dance; and as I was given to understand it was principally on my account, I could not do less than endeavour to please by jumping, for dance I could not'.

As for the Indians, he was, generally speaking, on friendly terms with them and, as we have seen, often employed them as guides or canoeists. They called him King George's Chief or the Grass Man because of his preoccupation with plants. Some of them thought he was a great medicine man with the power of turning people into grizzly bears. They were particularly impressed by his marksmanship, having no conception of shooting on the wing. Stung by an Indian brave who said that no chief of King George could shoot like him (or for that matter sing the death song or perform the war dance), Douglas tells us,

I charged my gun with swan shot, walked up to within forty-five yards of a bird that was perched on a dead stump, threw a stone to raise him, and when flying brought him down. This had the desired effect: many of the Indians placed their right hands on their mouths – the token for astonishment or dread. But the brave in question had still a little confidence in his abilities and offered me a shot at his hat; he threw it up and I carried the whole of the crown away, leaving only the brim.

After that the entire tribe wanted to buy his gun.

But not all Indians were friendly. On one occasion a band of them began pillaging the boats of Douglas and a party of fur-traders he was with. Pulling an arrow from his quiver, an Indian was about to shoot one of the white men when Douglas strode in among them with his loaded gun and settled matters. Again, when he was gathering cones of the fir-tree that is named after him – he actually shot some of the cones down with buckshot, they were so high up – he was rudely interrupted by a hostile band who 'endeavoured to destroy me', as he euphemistically put it, and he had to beat a hasty retreat on horseback.

More nerve-racking was an incident in the Blue Mountains near 'Lewis and Clark's' river. Angered by a verbal slip on the part of an interpreter, a band of seventy-three Indians, dressed in nothing but eagle head-dress and painted red, black, white and yellow, stormed into Douglas's camp with guns cocked and every bow strung. In the nick of time Douglas and his companions roused themselves and confronted the intruders in an elaborate war of nerves. After a great deal of palaver (that would not have disgraced a modern orator, Douglas observes sarcastically) peace was restored, the only casualty being the interpreter who had a handful of his long jet-black hair torn out by the roots.

Danger from Indians constantly threatened, even if in the end it usually petered out.

In the evening about three hundred men in their war garments danced the war dance and sang several death songs, which to me imparted an indescribable sensation. The following day seventeen canoes of warriors, nearly four hundred men, made their appearance, when, after several harangues, hostilities were for the present suspended.

Tobacco was always an essential on such occasions and not even the pettiest matter could be discussed without a preliminary puff at a pipe. Douglas never minded giving away tobacco when he had it to spare, but any thieving speedily brought the old Douglas to the surface, and this went for articles other than tobacco. It is always more pungent to let him recount an incident in his own words:

While eating my food an Indian who was standing alongside me managed to steal my knife, which was tied to my jacket by a string, and being the only one used for all purposes I was loth to part with it. I offered a reward of a little tobacco for its recovery, without

94

Men have had mountains, dustbins, instruments of execution, railway engines, motor cars, named after them. But few have had such a stately memorial as David Douglas, whose name is perpetuated by the Douglas fir. In its native habitat of western America, this tree can attain a height of well over two hundred feet. By comparison, Nelson's Column in Trafalgar Square is 182 feet high. (Left) Fir cones brought back by Douglas.

95

Lupinus polyphyllus ; var. albiflorus.

According to the Vocabulary of Flowers, often quoted in Douglas's time, the lupin represented Veraciousness and Dejection. Veracity Douglas always possessed. Dejection came upon him frequently, for he was continually forcing himself to the limits of physical endurance. This wild lupin, in an illustration from the *Botanic Magazine* of 1831, is one of the scores of specimens Douglas brought home.

the only hazards he encountered. Some were more in the nature of discomforts: he started to complain about ants biting him in an 'Indian hall'. Far worse, he discovered, was 'an indescribable herd of fleas', which forced him to sleep in the open air. Affronts to his person, however, were as nothing compared with damage to his precious specimens – as when, to his fury, 'rats', as he calls them, though they were probably prairie dogs, devoured all the seeds he had laboriously collected, damaged a number of plants and, adding insult to injury, first made off with his razor and soap-brush and even tried to sneak his inkstand. This was too much: he woke up and gave the marauders the contents of his gun.

Grizzly bears, Douglas soon appreciated, were not to be tampered with. Near the Umpqua River in Oregon one of his companions almost stumbled on a bear, loosed off a panic-stricken shot and tried to climb into a nearby tree. The grizzly grabbed him, but fortunately the man's home-made clothes gave way – blanket, coat and trousers were torn off him. More or less naked, he managed to scramble higher up and shout for help – 'this species of bear cannot climb trees', Douglas drily observed after rescuing the man.

On another occasion a white trapper in his party was attacked by a wounded 'buffalo'. He was gored and tossed several yards, ribs broken, thigh laid open to the bone. He saved himself by clutching hold of the buffalo's curly 'wig', while the rest of the party gazed on helplessly, having run out of ammunition. Night falling and in any case the man being presumed dead, he was abandoned till morning, when David Douglas came on the scene in time to prevent the 'half breeds' from firing off a salvo at random. For the bull was still standing near its victim, which it merely sniffed elaborately, then turned the man over and walked off. The man's wounds were grievous enough, but his life had been saved by a sealskin pouch which protected his heart and lungs. 'My lancet being always in my pocket like a watch,' says the ever-resourceful botanist, 'I had him bled and his wounds bound up, when he was carried to the boat; gave him twenty-five drops of laudanum and procured sleep.'

Tired out at Fort Assiniboine Douglas fell asleep at the camp-fire and badly burnt his big toe and blanket. He records his appearance during the same period: 'I had one shirt, a pair of leather trousers, an old straw hat, neither

effect. At last I commenced a search and found it secreted under the belt of one of the knaves. When detected he claimed the premium, but as he did not give it up on the first application, I paid him, and paid him so well, with my fists, that he will, I daresay, not forget the *Man of Grass* for some days to come.

Hostile or even thieving Indians were far from being

shoe nor stocking nor handkerchief of any description, and perhaps from my careworn visage had some appearance of escaping from the gates of death. Every two or three hundred yards I was obliged to call for a rest.'

Rivers had to be crossed and recrossed many times.

Rose at daylight and had my horses saddled, and being desirous of making the most of my time I took no breakfast further than a little dried meat and a drink of water, and proceeded on my journey at five o'clock. At twelve noon reached a small rapid river called the Barrière which took up an hour in crossing. As there were no Indians near the place, we had to choose either making a raft or to swim. As the latter was the easier method, and all of us good water-men, we unsaddled the horses and drove them in. I made two trips on my back, one with my paper and pen, the other with my blanket and clothes, holding my property above water in my hands.

At another river, one of his horses, eager to drink, fell in head foremost. Douglas and his Indian guide tried repeatedly to drag it out with ropes, but they were too weak from hunger. Douglas was in the act of putting powder in the pan of his pistol to end the animal's misery, when the Indian, angered at chafing his hand on the rope, 'struck the poor creature on the nose a tremendous blow with his foot, upon which the animal reared up and placed its forefeet on the steep bank, whereupon the Indian immediately caught him by the bridle and I pricked him in the flank with my pen-knife, and not being accustomed to such treatment, with much exertion he wrestled himself from his supposed grave'.

Beset by spectacular storms, avalanches, treacherous ice, unexpected chasms, Douglas had his tumbles: he once fell down a precipice, lay for five hours unconscious and, when he came to, bled himself as the most efficacious treatment and then took a bath in the nearby river. Raging torrents were a constant hazard. On one occasion, his Indian canoe was overwhelmed by a sudden river-surge. Douglas lost all his provisions, but this mattered hardly at all: the main thing was that he contrived to salvage his papers and botanical specimens. Conditions were always made worse by melting snow, when rivers were much swollen. At one place on the Kettle River, near the present border between Canada and the United States, the water was fourteen feet deep and six hundred yards wide in stretches. The boat shot downstream like an arrow from a bow and Douglas's guide, at that time a Canadian voyageur, proposed to shoot 'The Narrows of Death' as the rapids were graphically named. The hellish waters made Douglas confess his 'timidity', an unlikely quality in him, and he chose to make his way along the rocky bank. But he spoke with admiration of the skill shown by the Canadians as they paddled through the roaring chaos, evading by a hair's breadth the jagged rocks which 'they approach and pass with an indescribable coolness, cheering themselves on with an exulting boat-song'.

The adventures of this truly intrepid naturalist were countless. For many they alone would have been more than enough. But all this time Douglas had been carrying out his botanical work, at which his achievements were as prodigious as his adventures. He returned home in 1828 to universal acclaim, not merely from the Royal Horticultural Society. The Linnean Society, the newly formed Zoological Society and the Geographical Society all elected him a Fellow, for his findings had been far more wide-ranging than botany alone. His fame spread across the world – and, for example, the Tsar of Russia gave his support to a proposal that Douglas should make an expedition across Alaska and Siberia and back by way of the Urals and Russia (Alaska was only purchased from the Russians in 1867). In London, Douglas was fêted wherever he went, for here was a man who had helped to open up the almost fabulous Far West, had climbed the highest mountains in the Rockies, trekked across Canada to Hudson Bay and even journeyed awhile with Sir John Franklin (described by Douglas as 'a good man').

But after the rugged wilderness life David Douglas had led in North America, it is not surprising that a man of his character did not take kindly to 'civilized' society. Moreover, honoured though he was, he had been meagrely paid by his employers. In addition, he was angered at finding that many of his natural history specimens, which he had so perilously obtained and conscientiously dispatched, had been neglected and allowed to spoil. He quarrelled extensively, with Sabine, the Royal Horticultural Society's secretary, even with Sir William Hooker, who summed it up in these words: 'His temper

Hooker's administrative duties did not impede his extensive editorial and research work. Among his prolific writings was *Icones plantarum*, from which this illustration comes. This plant, *Argyroxiphium sandwichisama*, was brought back by Douglas from the Sandwich Islands.

became more sensitive than ever, and himself restless and dissatisfied; so that his best friends could not but wish as he himself did, that he were again occupied in the honourable task of exploring North-West America.'

So in 1829 Douglas set out again for the West Coast, and never returned to England. He was commissioned variously by the Royal Horticultural Society, the Zoological Society, the Royal Navy (who valued his help in map-making) and the Hudson's Bay Company. The pattern of his adventures continued much as before as he continued his work in the Columbia region. But all was far harder for him now, since his previous expedition had left him exhausted. Still barely thirty, people took him for at least fifty. He was bitterly disappointed when the Tsarist-backed project eventually came to nothing. He went south to California where, amidst his botanical labours, he was relaxed enough to remark that 'the ladies are handsome, of a dark olive brunette, with good teeth, and the dark fine eyes which bespeaks the descendants of Castille'.

Nevertheless, after eighteen months in California, he went off in 1833 to the Sandwich Islands, alias Hawaii. He was happy here too, intrigued by the natives' concept of beauty, which consisted of being as fat as possible, and overawed by the volcanic magnificence of Mauna Kea. But with funds running short he decided reluctantly in June 1834 that he must sail for home in the next available English ship. However, before he set off for Honolulu, he had offered to show a visiting missionary something of the island's natural charms. A meeting was arranged and in due course Douglas set off, alone except for his dog Billy, to meet his new acquaintance.

The rendezvous never took place.

Over the years, a number of domestic cattle had gone wild in the islands. They were regularly hunted by American settlers, mainly by means of pit-traps. Two or three pits would be dug around the perimeter of a natural watering-hole, and this was fenced in except for narrow entrances near the pits themselves which were concealed with foliage and soil. Some time after Douglas had said goodbye to his previous night's host, an ex-convict named Ned Gurney, the latter's Hawaiian servants heard the unmistakable noise of a bull thrashing and bellowing in one of their master's traps.

Approaching the trap, they came across the dog Billy howling dismally as he stood guard over a bundle of clothes. When they reached the edge of the pit they saw that under the enraged and terrified bull lay the body of a man, badly gored, almost unrecognizable. But because of Billy, they knew instantly that it was David Douglas. Nobody was ever certain of what exactly happened. Some even suspected Gurney. But the most likely explanation was that the bull had already fallen into the trap and David, his curiosity aroused by the animal's frantic bellowing, had gone to look, lost his footing on the muddy brink, and tumbled in. It was a ghastly end for one who had so often passed through 'danger's troubled night' in that distant country which he had made so much his own.

11 Out of Africa

In 1903 there died in St Petersburg a man who had for some years been travelling extensively in Scandinavia, had made a serious study of the Viking age, and written a popular travel book called *Land of the Midnight Sun*. This was all far removed from the fever-haunted forests of West Africa from which, forty years before, he had brought news that startled the Western world. His name, Paul Belloni du Chaillu, is now synonymous with the gorilla, and it seems incredible that this 'naturalist', who confirmed the existence of a hitherto almost mythical creature, lived on into the twentieth century.

The gorilla had not of course been known by that name, though there had been rumours of its existence for many hundreds of years – ever since the fifth century B.C., when Hanno's Carthaginian adventurers had reported seeing a fearsome manlike creature near the coast of Sierra Leone. Fresh reports started circulating at the end of the sixteenth century, at a time when, as a result of the slave-trade, the west coast of Africa was becoming increasingly known. In 1590 an English seaman, Andrew Battel, wrote or dictated an account of an enormous ape, which he dubbed the Pongo. Though it was of giant stature, it had the form of a man, the only difference being that its legs had no calves – a nice touch of verisimilitude. Its face, hands and ears were hairless, while its body was moderately covered with a dun-coloured pelt. When the creature walked, it did so upright, clasping its hands at the back of its head. It slept in trees, constructed a shelter from the tropical rain, and was entirely a vegetarian. It possessed no intellect, said Battel loftily, and acted only by instinct.

Travelling through the forest, people would build fires at night and, on their departure in the morning, groups of pongos would come and huddle round, gazing at the embers until these faded, for they did not have the wit to stoke the fire. But in spite of their vegetarianism, the pongos sometimes trailed those same African travellers and waylaid them, killing them out of hand. Moreover, if they chanced upon a herd of elephants, they would fall on the unfortunate pachyderms and beat them with their fists and with sticks until the elephants were forced to run off, trumpeting in understandable dismay.

For long Battel's account of the Pongo was regarded in much the same light as Marco Polo's report of the Giant Roc, which could snatch up a couple of elephants

Pliny wrote: 'In the deserts of Africa you will often meet with fairies appearing in the shape of men and women, but they soon vanish away like fantastical illusions. Nature delights to set us a-wondering at such strange mysteries.' Du Chaillu was one of the men irresistibly drawn to seek out those mysteries.

'Passing the Streams of Fire,' says the report of Hanno's voyage, 'we came to a bay called the Horn of the South where there was an island full of wild men and women with hairy bodies, whom the interpreters called "Gorillas". All the wild men escaped, being able to climb the precipices, but three women, who bit and scratched those who took them, were killed, after which we flayed them, and took the skins to Carthage.'

in its talons, fly off with them into the sky, then drop them to earth, in order more conveniently to feast on the smashed-up remains. Buffon, it is true, in his worthy thirty-six volume *Histoire naturelle* (1749–88), was inclined to give Battel the benefit of the doubt, sensing that there were one or two authentic stitches among the embroidery. But the great Cuvier of Napoleonic times dismissed the story as a mere sailor's yarn, one likely to be rewarded by spellbound listeners with a pot of ale. However, rumours concerning the mysterious great ape persisted.

Tangible evidence of this creature did not materialize until 1847 when Dr Savage, an American missionary in the Gabon, produced a drawing of its skull, clearly showing prominent bony crests over the eye-sockets, one of the characteristics distinguishing the gorilla from the chimpanzee. The zoologists became even more excited when this was followed up by far more important evidence – two actual skulls of the almost legendary species. One of these was sent to the United States, following which the Boston *Journal of Natural History* published a tentative description of the newly discovered ape, under the name of *Troglodytes gorilla*.

If the skulls had excited scientific circles, an infinitely greater sensation was caused in 1851 when a Captain Harris presented a complete gorilla skeleton to the Royal College of Surgeons. Here was incontrovertible evidence that this was an entirely different species from the chimpanzee, with which it had hitherto been confused. It was accorded the scientific title of *Gorilla savagei* – not as it might seem on the face of it an indication of how the animal was for long regarded, but in honour of Dr Savage.

There now entered on the scene the 'Gorilla Man', Paul du Chaillu himself. Born in Paris around 1831, du Chaillu emigrated as a young man to the United States and, like his compatriot Jean-Jacques Audubon before him, became an American citizen. His association with West Africa came about through his trading activities, but when he read Dr Savage's account of his discoveries he turned overnight into a fervent hunter-cum-naturalist.

Du Chaillu could not have chosen a better moment for his discoveries. Throughout the ages, from the days of antiquity to those of the blackbirders and Mungo Park, curiosity about the 'Dark Continent' had mounted, and there was now an insatiable appetite for information about it. Livingstone had set out on the first of his epic adventures; Speke and Burton were searching for the source of the Nile. Du Chaillu proceeded to whet that appetite even further: what was more, his sensational book was to appear at a time when the scientific world was being rocked by Darwin's *Origin of Species*.

In 1856 du Chaillu started out on his famous expedition into the Gabon, and a few years later he set the world agog with his *Adventures in the Great Forest of Equatorial Africa and the Country of the Dwarfs*, a work that was to give rise to scores of lurid romances through succeeding generations. Undoubtedly du Chaillu made many genuine discoveries, and certainly he added to the store of natural history. He it was who first made known the strange otter-shrew, one of the most extraordinary members of Insectivora, resembling a medium-sized ot-

The gorilla nowadays is on the endangered list. Many are killed for food by Africans; many are collected in the interests of medical research and the pharmaceutical industry. But the greatest danger is encroachment on the gorilla's habitat by agriculturalists and pastoralists.

Chimpanzees are Man's closest relatives among the animals. They live mainly in Central Africa, and in groups of about fifty they will roam many miles through the tropical forest in search of food. Mostly they travel through the swaying branches, hurling themselves from tree to tree, but every now and then they descend to the ground and walk with long arms dangling, supporting themselves on their knuckles.

ter but which, instead of hunting for fish, probes among mud and stones for crustaceans with the aid of its sensitive, elongated and swollen muzzle armed with long bristles. He also recorded the 'Nshiego-mbouvé', or bald chimpanzee, which was eventually acknowledged as a subspecies. This creature was subsequently observed to include in its diet living animal food, an observation confirmed a century later by Jane Goodall when she obtained conclusive proof that chimpanzees are carnivorous as well as eating fruit, which is their main diet.

Inevitably these and other trophies fell to du Chaillu's gun ('I succeeded in bagging several specimens'; 'I shot it in the water'; 'Today I killed a remarkable animal'), but it was his accounts of the gorilla that aroused the keenest interest – and controversy. It is not known whether he had come across Purchas's *Pilgrimages of the World* (1613) in which Battel's description had appeared, but he repeats some of the old salt's yarns, such as that about gorillas clubbing elephants unmercifully, even though he mildly scoffs at them. But his book in general contains many instances of the gorilla's alleged ferocity.

The underbush swayed rapidly just ahead, and presently before us stood an immense male gorilla. He had gone through the jungle on all fours, but when he saw our party he raised himself erect and looked us boldly in the face. He stood about a dozen yards from us, and was a sight I think I shall never forget. Nearly six feet high, with immense body, huge chest, and great muscular arms, with fiercely glaring large deep grey eyes and a hellish expression of face, which seemed to me like some nightmare vision; thus stood before us this king of the African forest.

He was not afraid of us. He stood there, and beat his breast with his huge fists till it resounded like an immense bass-drum, which is their mode of offering defiance; meantime giving vent to roar after roar. The roar of the gorilla is the most singular and awful noise heard in these African woods. It begins with a sharp *bark*, like an angry dog, then glides into a deep bass *roll* which literally and closely resembles the roll of distant thunder along the sky, for which I have sometimes been tempted to take it where I did not see the animal. So deep is it that it seems to proceed less from the mouth and throat than from the deep chest and vast paunch.

His eyes began to flash fiercer fire as we stood motionless on the defensive, and the crest of short hair which stands on his forehead began to twitch rapidly up and down, while his powerful fangs were shown as he again sent forth a thunderous roar. And now truly he reminded me of nothing but some hellish dream-creature – a being of that hideous order, half man, half beast, which we find pictured by old artists in some representation of the infernal regions. He advanced a few steps – then stopped to utter that hideous roar again – advanced again, and finally stopped when at a distance of about six yards from us.

At that point, just as he began another of his roars, beating his breast in rage, we fired and killed him, and with a groan which had something terribly human in it, and yet was full of brutishness, he fell forward on his feet.

No doubt acting as the inspiration for Edgar Rice Burroughs's *Tarzan of the Apes*, published fifty-eight years later, du Chaillu included instances of women being abducted by this 'satyr-like creature'.

The women have a lively fear of the terrible gorilla, in consequence of various reports of women having been carried off by the fierce animal. Two women were walking through the woods when suddenly an immense gorilla stepped into the path, and, clutching one of them, bore her off in spite of the screams and struggles of both.

Sometimes men were captured and taken prisoner. But they were usually set at liberty by the gorilla, after suffering nothing more drastic than having their nails torn out. That was mild treatment compared with what the gorilla often meted out, according to du Chaillu's contemporary, the anatomist Richard Owen.

Negroes when stealing through shades of the tropical forest sometimes become aware of the proximity of one of these frightfully formidable apes by the sudden disappearance of one of their companions, who is hoisted up into the trees, uttering, perhaps, a short choking cry. In a few minutes he falls to the ground, a strangled corpse.

Du Chaillu claimed that it was his good fortune to be the only white man who could speak of the gorilla from personal knowledge. Certainly his books and lectures caused a sensation. He was given a hero's welcome in America, a standing ovation by the Royal Geographical Society in London, and was in general the talk of the town. But there were many who disputed his veracity. One of these was an English naturalist, Winwood Reade, best known as an Egyptologist and author of *The Martyrdom of Man* (1872). He was so sure the French-American was a latter-day Baron Münchausen he hurried out to the Gabon to put things right. In his *Savage Africa* he categorically denied that du Chaillu could ever have set eyes on a living wild gorilla. But it may be that Winwood Reade was piqued by the fact that he himself failed to get a glimpse of the animal: one he was convinced he was tracking inconveniently vanished before he could catch sight of it. Others to cast doubts on du Chaillu were members of a German expedition which, some years later, completely failed in their object of locating the species. Moreover, it was said that the gorilla skins purchased from du Chaillu by the British Museum showed that all the animals concerned had been killed by means of weighted spears. This was a common trapping method (described by David Livingstone in his *Narrative of an Expedition to the Zambezi*, 1865), in which a heavy block of wood, with a metal harpoon or lance attached to it, was suspended from a branch overhanging a game-trail. A trigger mechanism consisting of a rope of lianas would be set off by a passing animal, into whose back the four-foot blade plunged, driven by the log.

Be that as it may, du Chaillu certainly came in contact with young gorillas. Subsequent to his 'bagging' his first gorilla, he records that some African hunters who were working for him captured a young gorilla, after slaying the mother. Its acquisition was the greatest moment of his life; though we might have expected, rather, that his awesome encounter with that 'hellish dream-creature' would have taken pride of place in his experiences. His exultation knew no bounds when he saw 'the struggling little brute' frog-marched into the village. All the hardships, fever and hunger and peril that he had endured were rewarded in that instant.

Joe, as the young gorilla was dubbed, was confined in a hastily built cage, from which he promptly escaped, causing great mayhem. Du Chaillu complained that he had never seen a more morose or worse-tempered animal than Joe. After being roughly manhandled by the entire camp, poor Joe was now chained up securely. 'Ten days after he was thus chained,' du Chaillu notes, with a slight air of surprise, 'he died suddenly.'

Du Chaillu himself admitted subsequently that there were discrepancies in his claims. The frontispiece of his book proved to be a copy of an illustration of the gorilla in the Musée de Paris. His picture of the skeleton of his gorilla was betrayed by a bone fracture as being a copy of a skeleton in the British Museum. But perhaps the most obvious discrepancy in his claims about his encounters with gorillas was his falling for the old tales of the animal's ferocity, including its actual killing of people and bending of their firearms. This was pure fantasy, yet the legend continued for many years to come, and even the *Oxford English Dictionary* still refers to the gorilla as having 'a reputation for fierceness'. Maybe du Chaillu was led astray by his Gallic temperament and simply exaggerated the characteristic bluff-charge of the gorilla as a real attack. On the other hand, the faults of hyperbole may have been prompted by his original publisher. It has been alleged not only that the publisher rejected the first draft of the book because it was not sensational enough, but also rewrote it himself to ensure that it was sufficiently hair-raising.

The old conventional attitude to the gorilla has of course been completely rejected by modern zoologists, notably the American George Schaller who spent many months in the Albert National Park of the Congo (Zaïre), where he lived in remarkably intimate contact with family groups of gorillas. He wrote that not once had they shown ferocity or even simple anger towards him. On the contrary, they had felt so secure in his presence that they continued their daily routine even to the extent of sleeping beside the tree in which he had perched himself. Right from the start he noted that the gorillas had an extremely placid nature not easily stirred into excitement. However, on one aspect of the gorilla Schaller and du Chaillu do agree. Schaller admitted that

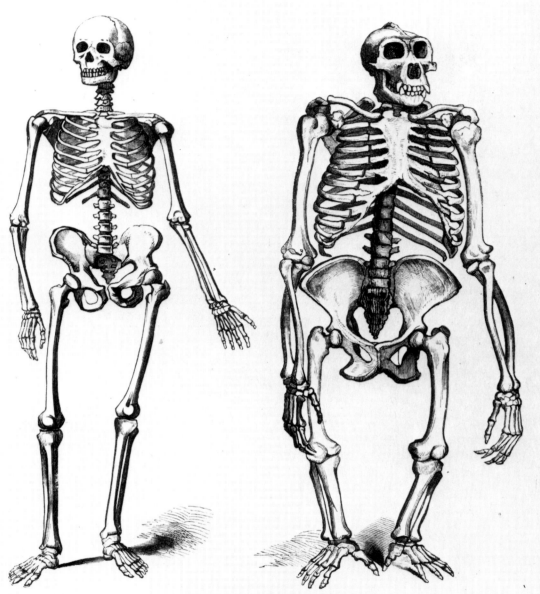

Skeletons of Man and the Gorilla.*

Man has	The Gorilla has
12 (and sometimes 13) pairs of ribs.	13 pairs of ribs.
7 cervical vertebræ.	7 cervical vertebræ.
12 dorsal (and sometimes 13) vertebræ	13 dorsal do.
5 lumbar (sometimes 4) do.	3 lumbar do.

Before becoming deeply interested in the gorilla, Carl Akeley worked as a hunter-collector. Here he is seen cuddling his victim, though in his day it was still fashionable to be photographed with a triumphant foot on one's 'bag'.

(Opposite) Another Akeley 'souvenir', "The Old Man of Mikeno", a portrait bust of his first gorilla, now in the American Museum of Natural History, New York.

he never got used to the shattering roar of the adult male. The sheer, abrupt explosion of it always made him want to run. But at least he had the consolation of noting that other gorillas were equally unnerved by it.

It is a pity that du Chaillu should have damaged his case by quite needlessly drawing the longbow, for as Schaller has said, he was basically a competent and reliable observer. His account of gorillas remained one of the most accurate for a hundred years, in fact until Schaller came along. For those other earlier 'gorilla men', R.L. Garner and Carl Akeley, had not completely thrown off the old ideas. Garner, evidently impressed by du Chaillu's warnings of the gorilla's ferocity, had the bizarre idea of building himself a strong iron cage. In this he sat hopefully, protected against all the terrors of the African forest; but, alas, no gorillas came to stare at him.

Carl Akeley, a naturalist and sculptor, originally went out to the Belgian Congo in 1921 to shoot gorillas for the

American Museum of Natural History in New York. He started off with the attitude that any 'white man who will allow a gorilla to get within ten feet of him without shooting is a plain darn fool'. However, he presently altered his opinion so much that he persuaded the Belgian Government to turn the gorilla's main homeland into the Albert National Park, where, incidentally, Akeley lies buried.

Undoubtedly du Chaillu blazed a trail, as we might say, into the African forest and stimulated an interest that has never flagged since. He brought to light – indeed, into the limelight – a near-fabulous animal, one of Man's most interesting relatives, and one of Africa's many prodigies. To illustrate how attitudes, through intimate study and observation, have altered over generations, here is an extract from Schaller's *The Year of the Gorilla* (1965). The contrast with some of du Chaillu's more lurid passages speaks for itself:

Eight juveniles, females, and a silverbacked male ascended two trees to a height of thirty-five feet and squatted on the branches, looking me over. I was immediately impressed with the placid and amiable countenance of the silverbacked male. He sat peacefully in the crown of the tree, his large angular body seemingly out of place in this arboreal environment. This male had a predilection for climbing, and I dubbed him the Climber. He was an average-sized fellow with a rather harsh look about his face, for the lines of his mouth curved downward and the hairs on his chin were scraggly and unkempt. But the eyes beneath his beetling brows were unusually soft and warm. Once he shook a branch violently and once he beat his chest as if to intimidate me. Then he descended to a lower branch, beat his chest again, yawned, defecated, lost his balance and nearly fell, and finally climbed all the way down.

12 'Nor Iron Bars a Cage'

Even in the days when Man's chief concern with wildlife was as a source of hunting for sport, he hankered after the company of animals. It was not simply the company of his hawk that he needed, and the attendant excitement of swift wings swooping relentlessly on partridge or heron or hare; nor the company of his hounds baying after deer. Although for many generations Man regarded nature as consisting of four kingdoms, the human kingdom as entirely separate, he was forever curious about animals and early on must have realized instinctively how close he was to them. It may be that a passion for hunting is deeply implanted in human beings, yet equally there is a restless curiosity in us. And this curiosity has always manifested itself in relation to wild creatures.

One manifestation of our interest in animals is witnessed by zoos, which in one form or another have existed for centuries. At first these were little more than menageries, often composed of gifts exchanged between rulers on ceremonial visits. Three thousand five hundred years ago, Queen Hatshepsut of Egypt made a collection of animals, including giraffes, monkeys and leopards. She dispatched envoys far and wide in search of specimens. In the ninth century A.D., Charlemagne possessed a sizeable little zoo of lions, apes and an elephant. The elephant was a gift from Haroun-el-Raschid, Caliph of Baghdad. After it had died, one of its tusks was made into an enormous hunting-horn. According to legend, it was this ivory horn on which Charlemagne's nephew Roland blew his last despairing message as the rearguard of the Frankish army retreated before the Moors. He must have been a mighty man indeed to have set such an instrument to his lips.

Even William the Conqueror and his sons were enthusiastic keepers of wild animals, while Henry III of England went so far as to acquire a polar bear. He made the burgesses of the City of London pay for its upkeep. However, they seem to have kept the bear on short rations, for it is recorded that sometimes it went fishing for salmon in the Thames. As noted earlier, Frederick II was a keen zoo-man in his pursuit of knowledge. And Linnaeus's wealthy English patron, George Clifford, kept a private zoo at Hartecamp, with a variety of exotic animals, including tigers, apes, peccaries, tropical deer and wild forest hogs. Linnaeus was so impressed that later on he greatly expanded the zoo in the Uppsala Botanical

Linnaeus had a green tree boa in his zoo at Uppsala. This snake lives in Brazil, Bolivia and Guyana, and can attain a length of ten or eleven feet. Mainly it lies in ambush, beautifully camouflaged, on the lower branches of trees, in wait for birds.

Gardens. For that, he obtained peacocks and parrots, cassowaries, agoutis, even an orang-utan. His favourite was a raccoon named Sjupp which became a household pet, as did one of the parrots, which used to sit on Linnaeus's shoulder and warn him when it was dinner-time. But needless to say, Linnaeus's main interest in the zoo was scientific.

All this had been anticipated in ancient times by the Chinese, who had a very enlightened attitude towards the keeping of wild animals in captivity, particularly regarding their conditions. They established 'Parks of Intelligence', in which animals could roam freely yet be watched by people. While, as we have seen, Alexander the Great had a practical approach to his 'zoo'. He encouraged Aristotle to make a scientific study of the animals in it, and much of the latter's *Historia animalium* was based on his researches there.

In more modern times the French contributed greatly to the development of zoos for scientific purposes. Louis XIV established a zoo at Versailles and employed two artists to make an inventory, consisting of minia-tures painted on vellum of all the inmates. This royal

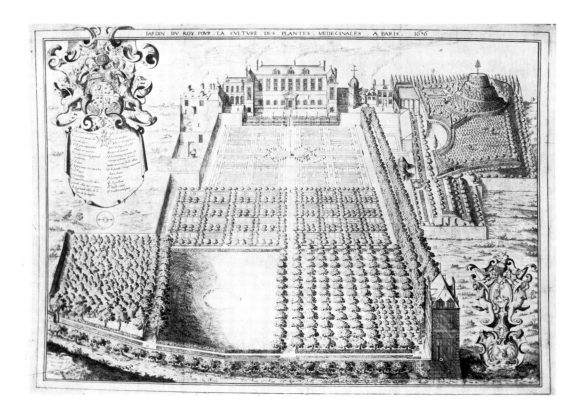

zoo presently expanded into the Jardin du Roi, which was superintended by Comte Georges Louis Leclerc de Buffon. One of his favourites was a chimpanzee with a liking for strawberries which Buffon trained him to eat with a fork. It was through being given the task of cataloguing the contents of the royal 'museum' that Buffon derived his ambitious idea of producing an account of the whole of nature. This eventually developed into his huge work, the *Histoire naturelle, générale et particulière*, which could be called the first successful attempt to gather together the hitherto isolated and disconnected facts of natural history into a generally intelligible form. But his fellow-naturalists did not like him and dubbed him the 'great phrasemonger'.

A notable advance in zoos was made in 1795, when the Jardin du Roi was reconstituted as the well-known Jardin des Plantes in Paris. This was done largely by the palaeontologist Baron Georges Cuvier in collaboration with three other French naturalists. The first of these was Louis Daubenton, who gave his name to a bat, also

A 'view' of the Jardin du Roi. Its best-known director was Buffon. He wrote picturesquely, prolifically and sometimes ponderously. Of the elephant he wrote: 'We must remember that his steps shake the earth, that he pulls up trees with his hand and with a blow of his body he can breach a wall.'

known as the water-bat, and which was evidently the creature Gilbert White was referring to when he wrote to Pennant about myriads of bats drinking on the wing like swallows when he was boating between Richmond and Putney on the River Thames. Better known was the Chevalier de Lamarck, a botanist, who, in common with Denis Diderot, had dabbled in the idea of a system of evolution, though he did not trespass too far into this tricky subject. The third, Geoffroy St Hilaire, had started off as a mineralogist. It was he who, in succession to Daubenton, was Curator of the Jardin des Plantes when it truly expanded into a zoo. This came about quite by chance. A posse of gendarmes turned up on the baron's doorstep with a collection of wild beasts – polar bears, mandrills, leopards – whose private owners had been refused permission to show them in public. Cuvier was to

Baron Cuvier enjoyed the patronage of the Duke of Württemburg, who arranged for him to attend the University of Stuttgart, where his biology teacher was Karl Friedrich Kielmeyer (1765–1844).

Before being associated with the foundation of the Regent's Park Zoo, Sir Stamford Raffles had had an illustrious career in the East Indies. He expelled the French from Java and governed the island brilliantly, only to see it handed back to the Dutch. Afterwards he founded the trading settlement which is now the city-state of Singapore.

become so enthralled with this collection, which helped him greatly in his study of comparative anatomy, that he refused an invitation from Napoleon to accompany the French expedition to Egypt in 1798 in the role of naturalist. St Hilaire went, however, and had to run the gauntlet of British guns when he was in Alexandria studying ichthyology.

Some thirty years later, in 1826, in consequence of the success of the Jardin des Plantes, the Zoological Society of London was founded. The enthusiasts behind this venture were Sir Humphry Davy, a world-famous scientist and President of the Royal Society, and Sir Stamford Raffles, famed for his association with Singapore and the East Indies. It was the latter's collection of Sumatran animals that formed the nucleus of the Regent's Park Zoo. But Raffles died before the enter-

(Above) The bear-pit: the zoo at its worst. But at least it was not as brutal as the bear-baiting with dogs which used to be a feature of every sizeable town in the past – as an alternative to bull-baiting, which only became illegal in England in the 1830s.

(Below) The elephant has always fascinated Man because of its immense size and strength, coupled with its tractability. Topsell called it 'Nature's great masterpiece'. He was not acquainted with nature's even greater masterpiece, the blue whale, the world's largest mammal!

prise was properly in train, but his memorial has endured.

The odd thing is that the entire British press ignored the new zoo – with one exception. The intellectual *Literary Gazette* remarked of it: 'Like too many of our modern associations and companies, it is extremely sonorous on paper; but, alas for the execution of the design – is it not altogether visionary?' Yet in spite of such pontifications, the zoo was an instant success. Within two years of its opening, a quarter of a million people were visiting the 'Regent's Park Menagerie' every year. This was a huge figure in days when the population of London was little more than one and a quarter million, and when transport for most people consisted at best of the horse-drawn omnibus.

The credit for turning menageries into zoos, albeit still with many shortcomings and drawbacks, must largely be accorded to Carl Hagenbeck, a revolutionary in his particular sphere. It was through his father's trade that Hagenbeck's involvement with wild animals came about. In turn, his father's interest had happened by chance. Herr Hagenbeck was a fishmonger in Hamburg. He employed a group of North Sea fishermen on contract to deliver their entire catch to him. One day in 1848 they turned up with six seals they had caught in their nets, thinking the animals might amuse their employer. They did. Herr Hagenbeck saw instantly the publicity these seals might bring him – and welcome revenue, too. He erected two enormous tubs outside his premises and charged a Hamburg schilling for a sight of these strange creatures of the sea, whose doleful voices had given rise to so many legends. So great was the fishmonger's success that he put the seals on show in Berlin. Thenceforth his fishmongering trade was conducted side by side with the modest menagerie he began to build.

Carl, born in 1844, grew up among the cheetahs and hyenas, monkeys and elephants that his enterprising father acquired. It was not surprising that he became the great entrepreneur of the zoological garden world. He lived at a time when Africa was being opened up, when du Chaillu was provoking Western imagination with his accounts of the gorilla, and when Livingstone, Burton, Speke, Samuel White Baker and Stanley were all making heroic contributions to men's knowledge of that continent. Though for less bloody reasons, people were as agog to see the wild beasts that emerged from Africa as

Carl Hagenbeck, doyen of zookeepers. He greatly influenced Sir Peter Chalmers Mitchell, who did so much for Regent's Park. One of Mitchell's most successful experiments was the construction of Monkey Hill, where for many years a colony of Arabian baboons lived in the open air.

were the plebs who had thronged the Roman circuses. An immense trade began to flourish, most of it bad. Carl Hagenbeck joined in. At first he relied on independent 'travellers', as he called them. But when one of them became ill and subsequently died, Hagenbeck had to hurry out to Egypt, as quickly as was then possible, in order to rescue the collection the man had assembled.

I shall never forget the sight which the hotel courtyard presented. Elephants, giraffes, antelopes and buffaloes were tethered to the palms. Sixteen tall ostriches were strolling loose. And in addition there were no fewer than sixty large cages containing a rhinoceros, lions, panthers, cheetahs, hyenas, jackals, civets, caracals, monkeys and many species of birds.

After this, Hagenbeck employed his own animal-catchers and travellers, who operated from the Sudan to Siberia. Man's curiosity exacted a heavy price. Quite apart from the inevitable distress the animals must have undergone, the task of transporting these ever-growing numbers of exhibits involved a bizarre piece of logistics. Hagenbeck paints a picture that puts one in mind of the Queen of Sheba setting out with lavish gifts for Solomon.

The caravan starts to march shortly before sunset. The larger animals are driven along by one or more attendants – a giraffe taking three persons, an elephant from two to four, an antelope two, and an ostrich, if large, also two. The smaller animals, such as young lions, panthers, wild pigs or birds, are carried in cages roughly constructed on the spot; and these cages are placed on the backs of camels. Right in the midst of our procession there marches a group of camels harnessed in pairs. Over the pack-saddles of each pair are laid two stout poles, and from these poles, between the two animals, hangs a large cage, made of strong rods bound together with strips of hide. Each cage contains a young hippopotamus, who, in spite of his youth, weighs with his cage well over a quarter of a ton. Each of these distinguished travellers requires a large party to wait upon him; for, in addition to the two camels which convey him along, six or eight others are required for carrying the water which he demands continuously throughout the journey, as also for the bath – made of tanned ox-hide – which he enjoys every day during the long halt. Hundreds of head of sheep and goats are driven along with the procession; the nanny-goats providing a constant supply of milk for the young animals, the remainder being used as food for the carnivores.

It is all much less complicated for a modern zoo-collector such as Bernhard Grzimek:

The okapi and the baby elephant, Dima, were completely unaffected by flying. Epulu the okapi calmly ate the fodder we gave him, and Dima thrust out her trunk every time we passed. The forest hogs slept peacefully. But the chimpanzees! When we first went aboard, and when the aircraft took off, they were very excited; but as we continued to climb, they became more and more torpid. Only Koki, the smallest of them all, ran round in lively fashion, seizing bananas wherever she could find them and clinging to our legs.★

★B. Grzimek, *No Room for Wild Animals* (1956).

Hagenbeck was of course a showman at heart. Some of his stunts included bringing, at different times, families of Lapps and their reindeer, Eskimos complete with sledges and kayaks, Somalis, Patagonians, and Nubian hunters, whose speciality in their homeland was hamstringing the animals they pursued. His great 'Cingalese' (Singhalese) caravan of 1884 included twenty-five elephants that plodded their stately way through Austria and Germany. He was an intimate of circus entrepreneurs such as the prestigious Phineas T. Barnum, who offered him a partnership.

Nevertheless, in spite of all the razzmatazz, Hagenbeck made a notable contribution to the development of modern zoo techniques. He did much to elevate the zoo from the old menagerie concept and stimulate an appreciation of the role we now see that it can play. One of his most important contributions was in dispelling the fallacy that wild animals had to be kept strictly protected against low temperatures. As so often happens, his discoveries in the field of acclimatization came about by chance. He was greatly impressed by seeing a captive chimpanzee playing in the snow. When it became cold it simply took itself off to a warmer spot near a stove. Again, soon after acquiring an Indian sarus crane, Hagenbeck had to go off on a business trip. While he was away, an intensely cold spell set in. He hurried back, expecting to find the crane frozen to death. Instead, the bird was in 'the most boisterous health', dancing and capering across its frost-bound paddock, shrilly expressing its pleasure.

It became apparent that exotic creatures could be kept in far better condition in the open air than in hot and stuffy houses. Needless to say, he made available to them shelters where they could take refuge from the worst weather; and in the case of antelopes he provided what he called natural heating. He allowed their dung to accumulate on the floor of the shelter to a foot in depth. It was covered daily with fresh straw, and this provided all the warmth the animals needed.

But, as he said, the fundamental law of acclimatization was to provide as much space as possible for the animals. It was not only healthy in itself for the animals to exercise properly, but the larger the space the greater the scope for creating a natural environment. 'I endeavour to consider the psychic as well as the physical condition of the

animals, so that they should forget, if possible, that they are prisoners at all.'

Revolutionary indeed was Hagenbeck's dispensing with bars in many cases. He introduced the trench system of protection as far back as 1896. As his first experiments were with lions, tigers and panthers, he had first to test their 'saltatory', or jumping, powers. Had he underestimated these, there might have been unpleasant consequences for the visitors.

He set up a stuffed pigeon on a branch ten feet above the ground and then let the big cats show their skill. Lions and tigers could manage only six feet six inches. Panthers were rather better. As for the long jump, ten feet from a standing start was the maximum. But in case any animal was cunning enough to attempt a flying start, Hagenbeck made the trenches twenty-eight feet wide. Elephants are more accommodating. They cannot jump and can only stride about two metres. That

'Animals are such agreeable friends,' said one of George Eliot's characters in *Mr Gilfil's Love-Story*, '– they ask no questions, pass no criticism.' Just as well at times, perhaps, or Man would end up in the dock.

has long been known in India where, for example, some places are protected by elephant trenches.

Another aspect of Hagenbeck's policy of providing animals with environment as nearly natural as possible was his use of 'panoramic scenery' – not always, though, to everyone's taste. He built huge artificial hills and rock formations made of wood, covered with a thin shell of concrete modelled over metal, with caves underneath for dens. This became the model for the innovatory Mappin Terraces of the Regent's Park Zoo in the days of Sir Patrick Chalmers Mitchell.

It may well seem strange to include zoo-keepers among pioneers of natural history. Therefore something need be said about the role of zoological gardens and the justification for them.

13 Captive but Free

The word 'zoo' still has unpleasant connotations. It is an ugly word to begin with and it still conjures up a vision of the old-fashioned bars-and-cage menagerie, implying the degradation and frustration of animals torn from the freedom of jungle, savannah or tundra. Yet, while ideally animals are best left alone in their natural wild habitat, it is a mistake to look upon every form of captivity as evil.

Provided always that their conditions are suitable in every way, from food to living-space, animals probably do not suffer any adverse effects from their captivity. Their chief concerns are food, procreation and the evasion of their enemies. The lion, which often seems bored in a zoo, would in the wild spend a great deal of time sleeping (he leaves most of the hunting to the lionesses in his 'pride'). The antelope in captivity has nothing to fear; in the wild it would be constantly on the alert for those same lions. In its natural state, the wildebeest about to calve is attended by hyenas ready to snatch its new-born young. The baby elephant is often in danger from the marauding tiger – or was until, alas, the tiger population of India shrivelled to around two thousand. Indeed, some animals may well enjoy more real freedom in zoos (this includes, of course, wildlife parks) than in their native habitat.

The main objection to the old-fashioned zoo was not only that it cabined, cribbed and confined the animals inside it. The cages also cut off people from the animals, not merely physically, for some sort of security is always necessary, but the bars created a mental barrier. They made people feel completely detached from the animals, depriving them of a properly sympathetic attitude towards them. Inevitably, cages and bars create in people's minds an image of animals simply as curiosities, laughable or grotesque as the case may be. Encouraging an awareness in people that they share the same origins and the same world as animals is one of the most important *raisons d'êtres* of the zoo, for not all of us can afford to go on safari tours.

Television has undoubtedly rendered an immense service by interesting people in wildlife. Brilliant films have given huge audiences amazing glimpses of wild creatures, from the dramatic migrations of caribou across the Canadian Barrens to the imperial eagle hunting in the Pyrenees, from the intimate life of the kingfisher in his

tunnel-nest to the strange world of the Namib Desert. Yet splendid though such films are, they cannot bring people into the live contact with animals that zoos can. Moreover, zoos help to demonstrate what people, through their money and interest, are being asked to conserve.

Mention has already been made of two important benefits to be derived from zoos, in reference to the Ancient Chinese and Alexander the Great: the opportu-

The zebra is perhaps the best example of natural camouflage. But it is of no avail against the lion, which ambushes it at drinking-holes. Man has not been exactly friendly, either. He exterminated the quagga, one of the zebra family, a hundred years ago.

San Diego is one of
the most famous zoos
in the world. Gorillas
are among the
endangered species
that have been
successfully bred in
captivity, the first
example being at
Columbus, Ohio, in
1956.

The European wild boar, pictured here, can weigh up to 350 pounds and be armed with tusks almost a foot long. It is virtually omniverous and its menu includes roots, beechmast, chestnuts, carrion, even snakes. Its range extends from western Europe to Central Asia.

nities afforded for educational and scientific study. An establishment such as the magnificent New York Bronx Zoo, with its emphasis on education, is but one example of this. And from the scientific viewpoint, the zoo can be of unique value as a living laboratory. In the past, the only possible place for studying subjects such as comparative anatomy was the zoo, as a naturalist like Cuvier appreciated. Nowadays, although much research, such as ecology, can and must be carried out in the wild, many other branches of natural history, including zoology itself, animal physiology, pathology and dietetics, can best be studied in the environment of the zoo.

It is in translocation and its concomitant, captive breeding, that zoos have an increasingly important role to play in helping to save species in danger of extinction. Attempts at translocation have gone on for a long time, as far back as the seventeenth century and possibly even further. Few people would regard Charles I as anything of a pioneer, but he was enterprising enough to attempt

In the Soviet Union the beaver has been rehabilitated through translocation. Every autumn live trapping takes place in the main Voronezh reservation, and in ten years more than five thousand beavers have been moved to different parts of the Russian Federation in an attempt to safeguard the future of the species.

the rehabilitation of the wild boar in England. Though James I had still hunted it at Windsor, the native species was already on the verge of extinction. So Charles I imported a number of animals from France (where even today the wild boar survives, in spite of persecution by hordes of trigger-happy 'chasseurs'), releasing them in the New Forest, Hampshire, that traditional royal hunting ground of English kings.

Charles's experiment was highly successful, for there was ideal feeding for the animals in the form of acorns and beechmast. But, records John Aubrey at the time, they were a terrible menace to travellers. Moreover, they were certainly resented by the local peasantry, who enjoyed the ancient right of pannage for pasturing their own domestic swine.

Successful though it was, however, this translocation enterprise was short-lived. The ensuing English Civil War and the breaking up of many estates led to the slaughter of any remaining wild boar all over the country. None the less, as late as 1683 an account book of Chartley Manor in Staffordshire showed that two shillings had been paid to the estate cooper for a fence to keep out 'wild swine'. In Westmorland there is a tradition that at about the same time one William Gilpin slew the last wild boar, his deed being commemorated in a bridge named after him.

During the Restoration, Charles I's attempt at rehabilitation was imitated by John Evelyn, diarist and champion of forestry. He introduced wild boar from Portugal and put them down in Surrey. This experiment also succeeded – only too well. The wild boar increased rapidly, for a wild sow will produce up to twelve marcassins in a litter. But, alas, they committed so much 'Spoyle' that they had to be destroyed. However, Mr Evelyn at least had the consolation of enjoying some 'incomparable bacon'. Evidently he found wild boar-meat more to his taste than that of the domestic porker. For in another context he had even praised the sweet or Spanish chestnut as being far more nutritious than 'rusty bacon', though he did add the rider 'especially for the peasantry'.

This enthusiasm for translocation continued. The wild boar was a popular subject partly because of its adaptability and high rate of breeding, and partly because it would have provided good hunting for the gentry. Towards the end of the eighteenth century, General Howe (not to be confused with the general of the same name who fought in the American War of Independence) brought over a number of wild boar from Germany and turned them loose in Alice Holt and Wolmer Forests in Hampshire, 'To the great terror of the neighbourhood'.

The general's efforts failed, not through any shortcomings on the part of the wild boar but because, as Gilbert White tells us, 'the country rose upon them and destroyed them'. But then, General Howe does seem to have been over-zealous for translocation. He went so far as to introduce wild buffalo, which suffered a similar fate at the hands of the allegedly outraged but probably gleeful rustics.

The beaver was another animal at whose rehabilitation the pioneers of translocation tried their hand. It is possible that the species still existed in Britain as late as the reign of Henry VIII. According to Hector Boece, or Boëthius, the sixteenth-century Scottish chronicler,

beavers were to be found in incomparable numbers in the region of Loch Ness. He reported that German traders journeyed as far as Inverness to purchase beaver skins, while in Wales at one time during the Middle Ages

> More famous long agone,
> than for the salmon's leap,
> for beavers Teivi was,
> in her strong banks that bred,

as Michael Drayton later wrote in his great topographical poem, *Polyolbion*, completed in 1622.

But, persecuted because of the warmth and comfort of its fur, as well as for its medicinal qualities, and adversely affected by deforestation, the beaver had inevitably disappeared from Britain. For many centuries the only remaining trace of one of the most intelligent and interesting wild animals was to be found in various place-names all over the country. Losleathan in Scotland, and Llostlydan in Wales, both speak of the 'broad-tail'. In Anglo-Saxon days the Yorkshire town of Beverley was Beoforleag, the beaver's lea. Beverege in Worcestershire, Bevercotes in Nottingham, and Beversbrook in Wiltshire, all bear witness to the beaver's once widespread presence.

In 1884, many centuries after the extinction of the beaver, the Marquess of Bute tried his hand at rehabilitation. He introduced French and American specimens to the Isle of Bute, off the south-west coast of Scotland. They set to work merrily and reshaped the noble lord's domain. But within fifteen years the colony of furry engineers had died out, largely for lack of material. It takes a large amount of timber to keep the beaver in business. He needs trees not only for his extensive dams but also for food.

More successful than the marquess's attempt was one started at about the same time at Leonardslee, near Horsham in Sussex. This translocated beaver colony thrived for sixty years, the last survivor dying in 1948.★ Most successful of all was the attempt that took place in Finland in the 1930s. Native beavers had been exterminated seventy years previously through excessive trapping. The experiment of rehabilitation was made largely with animals shipped from Canada, and the success of the project is revealed by the fact that the activities of the

---

★See R.S.R. Fitter, *The Ark in Our Midst* (1959).

virgin land. With much of the timber they built their log cabins, warmed their homes, made pitch and turpentine to protect roofs and walls. In many places they had to build roads of logs across swampland. Often the pioneers could not have survived without timber, for it was vital in the construction of blockhouses and palisades in the long and bitter struggle with the Indians who strove to defend their homeland. Staging-posts and strong-points, such as Fort Laramie and Fort Bridger, among many other key names in American history, were simply log-built stockades.

The plunder of the forests accelerated when, following the exploits of men like Lewis and Clark, and David Douglas, and Bonneville and Stuart, news spread of the incredible untouched forests on the West Coast. A 'green-gold' rush took place, surpassed only by the real gold-rush to California. It was said that one acre of West Coast forest contained more timber than five acres of the northern forest. Special trains were chartered to bring thousands of lumberjacks from the traditional timber-lands of the north-east, and they 'broke windows and kicked the doors of passenger coaches off their hinges, meanwhile bellowing to such effect that people wondered if a menagerie were passing'. Some timber firms in Maine even built their own ships to transport men and equipment round Cape Horn and up to Oregon and Washington State.

And still the new Americans were crowding into this land of almost fabulous promise. All of them had to be housed, warmed, provided with household furniture, carts and carriages and sledges and paddle-steamers and boats, and countless other articles of everyday life. The lumberjack became the most hard-worked figure in the country; he was scarcely able to keep pace with the demand for timber. It has been calculated that, between 1780 and 1930, 315 million acres of American forest-land were cut down.

Amidst this ravishing of nature, the desecration of the Great Plains, the mutilation of the forests, there were Americans who had already grown uneasy about it all. Splendidly vast this new land might be, but it was not limitless. As far back as 1791, William Bartram, son of John Bartram the botanist, had warned of the dwindling numbers of beaver. Fenimore Cooper, ardent exponent of the West as he was, added his experienced voice. Even

What Parkman achieved with his pen, Catlin did with his brush. These two sketches are from his working notebooks. The 'buffalo' bull is a ponderous but awesome creature and can stand six feet at the shoulder and weigh three thousand pounds. Attempts have been made in Poland and the U.S.S.R. to rehabilitate the European bison or wisent by means of American animals.

such an early folk-hero of Frontier days as Daniel Boone was aware of what was happening.

Sir [he said in a conversation with Audubon in 1810], what a wonderful difference thirty years makes in the country! Why, at the time when I was caught by the Indians, you would not have walked out in any direction for more than a mile without shooting a buck or a bear. There were then thousands of buffaloes on the hills in Kentucky; the land looked as if it would never become poor; and the hunt in those days was a pleasure indeed. But when I was left to myself on the banks of the Green River, a few signs only of deer were to be seen, and, as to the deer itself, I saw none.★

During his expedition to the Missouri, Audubon him-

★Quoted in Peter Matthiessen, *Wildlife in America* (1960).

The roaring waters of Yellowstone. This fantastic and unspoilt region of the United States was not properly explored until a century ago.

self became numbly aware of what was happening, as far certainly as the bison was concerned.

What a terrible destruction of life, as it were for nothing, or next to it, as the tongues only were brought in, and the flesh of these fine animals was left to beasts and birds of prey, or to rot where they fell. The prairies are literally *covered* with the skulls of the victims. Before many years, the Buffalo, like the Great Auk, will have disappeared.

And travelling through the Ohio Valley, Audubon was equally aware of the destruction of the forest. Everywhere he heard 'the din of hammers and machinery'. He warned that 'the greedy sawmills told the sad tale that in a century the noble forests would exist no more'.

Audubon's contemporary, George Catlin, who painted much of the American-Indian scene, also saw that 'many are the rudenesses in Nature's works which are destined to fall before the deadly axe and desolating hands of cultivating man'. And it could be said that Catlin was a pioneer in implanting in people's minds the conception of a national park, so that some of those 'rudenesses of Nature's works' could be preserved.

Journeying up the Missouri in 1832 on board the *Yellowstone* (he could not have foreseen how appropriate the name of the little river-boat would prove to be), Catlin had a pioneer vision. This was that all the endangered Indians, the buffaloes and the many other threatened wild creatures, as well as all the unspoilt land in which they existed, could be protected by the Government in a 'magnificent park'. What a wonderful and thrilling project this would be, he thought, for America to achieve – a national park, preserving nature in all its wild loveliness!

Thoreau echoed Catlin's thoughts:

Why should we not have our national preserves in which the bear and the panther, and some even of the hunter race, may still exist and not be 'civilized off the face of the earth' – our forests not for idle sport or food, but for inspiration and our own true recreation?

But Thoreau would have liked to see every civilized town and city with such a park; not the municipal kind of

park the word often brings to mind, but rather a wilderness in miniature of several hundred acres. Alas, even he could never have foreseen the population explosion that has taken place, the root cause of so many terrestrial problems of today.

Washington Irving, famed for many as the author of *The Legend of Sleepy Hollow*, had in another book, *Tour of the Prairies*, urged that a halt be called to the ruination of the country. He expressed the hope that the Rocky Mountains, 'where there is nothing to tempt the cupidity of the white man', might act as a barrier and remain a natural wilderness. Now, for long there had been rumours of an unspoilt tract of such wilderness on the north-west corner of what was to become the state of Wyoming. 'Blanket' Jim Bridger, one of the 'mountainy men' who had followed the Oregon Trail and afterwards acted as a scout for the American army against the Indians, had brought back news of magnificent canyons, boiling springs and spouting geysers. His tales, however, were written off as the mere fantasies of an old-timer who had pulled out his hip-flask too often. Yet, as the neighbouring region of Montana became more settled, the rumours increased of a strange wonderland of nature around the headwaters of the Yellowstone River. Human curiosity is an endemic fever, which leads to the exploring of planets and the limits of the mind. In the present case men could not rest easy until Jim Bridger's claims had been shown up as a 'magnificent myth', downright lies – or just possibly the truth.

The first serious attempt in unlocking the door of this incredible treasure-house of nature took the form of a private expedition. It was led by David Folsom who, accompanied by C.V. Cook and William Petersen, set out from Diamond City on the Missouri River on 6 September 1869. They were armed, we are told, with repeating rifles, Colt six-shooters, sheath-knives, with a double-barrelled shotgun for small game, and equipped with field-glasses, pocket compass, thermometer, and pro-

visions for a six weeks' 'trip', though they made it sound as if they were setting foot into the deep unknown.★

From the Missouri River they followed much of the course of the Yellowstone and began to thread their arduous way on horseback through the many groups of hot springs beyond the Grand Canyon, though they do not seem to have probed into this natural marvel. They pushed on farther up the river, past the significantly named Sulphur Mountain and Mud Volcano, too fascinated to turn back but apprehensive of what lay ahead. Eventually, after trekking through what was euphemistically termed 'toilsome' country across the mountains to Shoshone Lake, Wyoming, they came upon what is now known as Lower Geyser Basin. Here, wide-eyed and each one glad he had his companions as witnesses, they watched the Fountain Geyser in action and saw many other weird volcanic features of the dreamlike region. They ascended the Firehole River as far as Excelsior Geyser and Grand Prismatic Spring (all these names were given afterwards, needless to say), and then turned for home.

Not even stout Cortez and his men 'looked at each other with a wild surmise' greater than that of Folsom and his companions. Indeed, so utterly bemused were they by the marvels they had seen, 'they were on their return unwilling to risk their reputations for veracity by a full recital of them to a small gathering whom their friends had assembled to hear the account of their explorations'.

Fortunately David Folsom did write an account of his journey, which was published in the Chicago *Western Monthly*. This had an important influence in bringing about the official expedition in 1870. At the outset many prominent people were eager to join it. They hastily changed their minds, however, when it was known that Nez Percé Indians were on the war-path. Indeed, several years after the establishment of Yellowstone as a national park, the Nez Percé were still defying the Seventh Cavalry.

In the event, only nine men were willing to brave the

dangers in the interests of scientific discovery. They were led by General Henry Washburn, Surveyor-General of Montana, and Nathaniel Langford (who became first superintendent of the park), and escorted by Lieutenant Gustavus Doane of the Second Cavalry with a sergeant and four troopers. Even now, there was no mention of geysers or hot springs in the expedition's briefing. Indeed, some of the distinguished members of the party admitted to the general air of scepticism prevailing. But any doubts they had were to be abruptly and dramatically dispelled.

Through the mountain gap formed by the canyon [wrote Lieutenant Doane in a magazine article], and on the interior slopes some twenty miles distant, an object now appeared which drew a simultaneous expression of wonder from every one of the party. A column of steam, rising from the dense woods to the height of several hundred feet, became distinctly visible. We had all heard fabulous stories of this region, and were somewhat skeptical of appearances. At first it was pronounced a fire in the woods, but presently someone noticed that the vapor rose in regular puffs, as if expelled with great force. Then conviction was forced upon us. It was indeed a great column of steam puffing away on the lofty mountain side, escaping with a roaring sound audible at a long distance, even through the heavy forest. A hearty cheer rang out at this discovery, and we pressed onward with renewed enthusiasm.

The expedition discovered more and more treasures: the breath-taking beauty of Cascade Creek and Crystal Falls; the incomparable splendour of the Grand Canyon itself; followed by an almost stunning catalogue of ever-changing wonders. Even at last when, late in September, they were homeward bound, eager to tell their story and also to avoid the early winter sweeping down from the Rockies, Yellowstone still had another of its marvels to display. The dense forest concealed everything beyond the radius of a few hundred feet. All at once the explorers emerged into an open treeless valley.

Directly in front of them, scarcely two hundred yards away, a vertical column of water and steam was shooting upward a hundred and fifty feet in the air. The

★These details of the Yellowstone expeditions are based on Hiram Martin Chittenden's *Yellowstone National Park* (1895).

Portraits of General Washburn (below) and Lieutenant Doane who, together with Nathaniel Langford, carried out the first official exploration of Yellowstone. 'Blanket' Jim Bridger was amply justified by their discoveries.

Henry D. Washburn
1869

bright sunlight turned the clear water into a mass of glittering crystals, and a gentle breeze wafted the vast white curtain of steam far to the right across the valley. Thus it was that 'Old Faithful', as if forewarned of the approach of her distinguished visitors, gave them her most graceful salutation; and thus she bowed out the era of legend and fable and ushered the civilized world into the untrodden empire of the Fire King. Little wonder that our astonished travellers spurred their jaded horses and gathered round the wonderful phenomenon.

It was this Washburn–Langford–Doane Expedition, as it was commonly known, which led to the establishment of Yellowstone as a national park, $2\frac{1}{4}$ million acres in extent, approximating to a country the size of Cyprus. Other parks had been created earlier, notably the Yosemite Valley which was taken over by the state of California in 1864. But it was Yellowstone which undoubtedly saved the bison from extinction in the United States and, as Peter Matthiessen has put it in his excellent *Wildlife in America*, the park today

. . . harbors an impressive population and variety of great animals, including mule deer, elk, antelope, moose, bison, bighorn sheep, and black and grizzly bears [amidst] a glory of mountain meadows, alpine forest, geysers, canyons, torrents and a great blue lake pinned in by snow peaks of the Rockies.

George Catlin's dream had come true. He had indeed been a pioneer with his visionary idea. It was an idea that spread across the United States where the national park system now totals nearly 30 million acres, an area almost equalling that of the whole of England. And the idea has spread further, across the entire world, from Africa's Serengeti to Australia's Kosciusko, in Man's limping and belated attempts to protect nature. But not all the Yellowstones in the world could make amends for the slaughter and desecration that have been perpetrated. If Catlin and Thoreau and Audubon returned to the world today they would stand aghast at what they saw.

15 Best-selling Travel Book

Linnaeus, as we have seen, was a firm believer in the immutability of species. He believed implicitly in the biblical story of the Creation being achieved in six days. Yet it is an ironic fact that Linnaeus was indirectly responsible for the historic voyage on which Charles Darwin went in H.M.S *Beagle*; a voyage that was to provide him with the material and inspiration for the Theory of Evolution, which would have been anathema to the Swedish scientist. This was to rock the scientific and religious beliefs of the Victorian world, and make Darwin's name far more famous than Linnaeus's.

It was Linnaeus's practice of sending out his student-disciples far and wide to collect specimens from some of the most unwholesome corners of the tropics that inspired Sir Joseph Banks to accompany Captain Cook in the *Endeavour*. From then on, it became accepted practice for expeditions of discovery to carry among their personnel a naturalist or scientist. Edward Sabine going as astronomer with Parry in search of the North-West Passage, and Joseph Dalton Hooker accompanying Sir James Clark Ross on his 'Voyage of Discovery and Research in the Southern and Antarctic Regions', are but two notable examples.

Darwin was born in Shrewsbury in 1809 (the year Lamarck published *Philosophie zoologique*, his work on 'transformism', as the theory of evolution was called in France). Charles was the fifth of six children of Dr Robert Darwin and Susannah Wedgwood, daughter of the famous Josiah. In his autobiography Darwin described his father as the largest man he ever saw – more than six feet tall and weighing twenty-four stone. He also called him the kindest man he ever knew. At least he thought so as a boy, though later on he and Dr Darwin by no means saw eye to eye. But then neither had the doctor with his father, Erasmus Darwin, some of whose brilliance and breadth of interest must have been passed on to his grandson.

Erasmus Darwin, who has, not surprisingly, always been overshadowed by Charles, was a man of many parts. He practised as a physician in Lichfield, Staffordshire, where he gained a reputation for unorthodox but effective methods. But his interests extended far beyond doctoring. He was a Fellow of the Royal Society and an enthusiastic member of the famous Lunar Society, so called because it held its meetings at full moon

Erasmus Darwin thought the Industrial Revolution would herald in a paradise on Earth and at times he had recourse to verse:

Soon shall thy arm, unconquered steam! afar
Drag the slow barge, or drive the rapid car;
Or on wide-waving wings expanded bear
The flying chariot through the field of air.

Darwin, shown here with Lyell and Hooker, had good friends to counter-balance his enemies. In an earlier age Darwin would certainly have ended up alongside Galileo, persecuted by the Inquisition.

to make it easier for members coming from a distance. Those members, nicknamed the Lunatics, included such significant names as James Watt, Matthew Boulton, the chemist Joseph Priestley, Josiah Wedgwood himself, and Dr William Withering who discovered the use of digitalis, the drug made from dried foxglove leaves.

The range of Erasmus Darwin's ideas was quite amazing. He darted from a proposal for artificial insemination to a design for a water-closet, both equally revolutionary in their different ways. In *The Economy of Vegetation* (1791) he had, surprisingly in view of the book's title, tentatively put forward the notion of the 'big bang' theory of creation. He also mentioned the possibility of submarine exploration of the polar ice-cap and of air travel. But then even Dr Johnson had dilated on flying in

Prince Rasselas. Most interesting of all, in *Zoönomia*, Erasmus had vaguely discussed evolution.

With such a background, and of course with no less a luminary than Josiah Wedgwood as his other grandfather, perhaps it is not surprising that Charles Darwin eventually reached great heights. But it was not so at first. Nobody who knew him as a young man would have conceived of his name becoming a household word. 'When I left school I was for my age neither high nor low in it; and I believe that I was considered by all my masters and by my father as a very ordinary boy, rather below the common intelligence.' Shades of Linnaeus!

Nothing could have been worse for the development of his mind than Dr Butler's school at Shrewsbury. Apart from classics, nothing else was taught except a little ancient geography and history. It was all 'simply a blank'. But it could not have been altogether so. At least he became a devoted admirer of Gilbert White, whose *Natural History of Selborne* had a considerable influence on him. Already he was showing signs of discovering his ultimate bent by becoming an avid collector of natural history objects, an enthusiasm that never deserted him.

I will give you a proof of my zeal: one day, on tearing off some old bark, I saw two rare beetles, and seized one in each hand; then I saw a third and new kind, which I could not bear to lose, so that I popped the one which I held in my right hand into my mouth.★

Reaction was prompt. The outraged beetle im-

★Charles Darwin, *Autobiography* (1876).   139

The *Beagle* in Ponsonby Sound. 'A small family of Fuegians, who were living in the cove, soon joined our party round a blazing fire. We were well clothed and though sitting close to the fire were far from too warm; yet those naked savages, although farther off, were observed, to our great surprise, to be streaming with perspiration at undergoing such a roasting.'

mediately squirted a burning and unpleasant liquid into Darwin's mouth and the eager collector was forced to spit it out.

Rather like Linnaeus's father, Dr Robert Darwin decided that what was good enough for him was all right for his son. Charles should be a doctor, too. So to Edinburgh University Darwin went in 1825, to join his brother Erasmus who was already there. But Charles soon discovered that he was not cut out to be a medical man. Not only were the lectures abominably dull, but he blenched at and ran away from the operations he was obliged to witness. Justus von Liebig, the German chemist, did not discover chloroform until 1831 – the year Darwin went off in the *Beagle*.

But at least in Edinburgh he met Audubon, who had gone there to consult Home Lizars, the engraver. He also read a learned paper to the Plinian Society, and, of immense future practical use, received lessons in taxidermy from a Negro who had worked for Charles Waterton during his 'Wanderings'.

So atavistic are we in our attitudes that sheer physical bulk tends always to overawe us. In this respect Darwin was no exception. He was so awed by his father that he could not bring himself to tell him he did not want to be a doctor. He did not even go home during the vacations. It was left to his sisters to break the news to Dr Darwin, who had nurtured fond hopes of Charles taking over the practice. Doing a Linnaeus *père* in reverse, the doctor decided that if his son was too stupid to be a physician, he should become a priest.

The idea of Darwin entering the Church, to which his theories were in the course of time to deal such a staggering blow, is almost as ironical as Joseph Stalin training as a priest. Anyway, with the priesthood in mind, Darwin went to Cambridge at the age of nineteen. He was perhaps more likely to succeed in this new line, for 'I did not then in the least doubt the strict and literal truth of every word of the Bible and I soon persuaded myself that our creed must be fully accepted'. However, he considered his three years at Cambridge a waste of time. He was far keener on partridge shooting with 'some dissipated low-minded young men' than on pursuing his academic studies.

Nevertheless, he obtained a moderately good degree, and while in Cambridge Darwin made some influential friends, among whom were Adam Sedgwick, his professor of geology, and most particularly the Reverend John Stevens Henslow, professor of botany. The pulpit was still Darwin's chosen aim, but at that moment he happened to read Alexander von Humboldt's *Personal Narrative*. Spurred on by this book, and perhaps in an attempt to elude his ecclesiastical fate, he decided to set out on a private expedition to Tenerife. He even started to learn Spanish.

Fortunately for history, Professor Henslow had seen that Charles Darwin had far more aptitude for geology, botany and natural history in general than for the Thirty-nine Articles. At the time Darwin was arranging his jaunt to the Canary Islands, Henslow learned that Captain Fitzroy of the *Beagle* was soon to set out on another voyage of hydrographical survey and desired to take a naturalist with him, preferably a young man with private means. H.M.S. *Beagle* was a ten-gun sloop-brig of

235 tons, ninety feet long and twenty-four feet eight inches in the beam, and had been launched in 1820. She had already made a voyage to South America during the years 1826–30. Now she was fitting out for another voyage, of five years' duration.

Through Henslow's good offices the job was offered to Darwin. The offer nearly went by default, for Darwin turned it down; partly because he was not confident in his health, and partly because of paternal disapproval. 'If you can find any man of common sense who advises you to go,' said Dr Darwin, 'I will give my consent.' Fortunately that 'man of common sense' existed in the person of Dr Darwin's brother-in-law, Josiah Wedgwood II. 'Uncle Jos' even rode over forthwith to Shrewsbury to convince Robert Darwin that his son simply must take up this golden opportunity. Charles immediately rescinded his previous refusal and spent an anxious time waiting to hear if it was too late. Luckily for him the vacancy had not been filled. But now there was another obstacle. The aristocratic Captain Robert

Fitzroy, R.N., nephew of Viscount Castlereagh and descended, through a by-blow, from Charles II, did not approve of the shape of Darwin's nose. It was not forceful enough. It was not a nose of character. It was not the nose of a man who could put up with the hardships of five years in the confined quarters of a tiny brig voyaging in savage parts and desolate seas. Moreover, was it the nose of a man who would have to share the captain's cabin all that time? Finally, however, Captain Fitzroy withdrew these objections. Although he was undoubtedly a very difficult man at times, imperious, dogmatic, morose in turn, he must have had some tolerant side to his character.

Except during various land expeditions on the voyage, Darwin was to be cheek by jowl with Captain Fitzroy for an unconscionable time. Morning was the worst time for the captain. Darwin noted sadly that Fitzroy was then always suspicious, on the look-out for the slightest fault, and often in low spirits to the point of madness (like his uncle, Castlereagh, he eventually committed suicide).

These illustrations (opposite, above and previous page) are from Captain Fitzroy's narrative of his surveying voyages, companion to Darwin's *Journal of Researches*. Darwin wrote of the Fuegians: 'These poor wretches were stunted in their growth, their hideous faces bedaubed with white paint, their skins filthy and greasy, their hair entangled, their voices discordant, and their gestures violent. Viewing such men, one can hardly make oneself believe that they are fellow-creatures, and inhabitants of the same world.' Of the neighbouring Patagonians he was more tolerant: 'We had an interview at Cape Gregory with the famous so-called gigantic Patagonians, who gave us a cordial reception. Their height appears greater than it really is, from their large guanaco mantles, their long flowing hair, and general figure: on an average their height is about six feet; and the women are also tall; certainly the tallest race which we anywhere saw. Captain Fitzroy invited three of these giants on board to dine with us, and they behaved quite like gentlemen, helping themselves with knives, forks, and spoons.'

There were frequent brushes between the two men, for Fitzroy was an uncompromising fundamentalist, while Darwin's view of the Creation changed steadily during the course of the voyage. One illuminating sidelight not only on Fitzroy himself but on the times in general was the case of the three Fuegian Indians – a woman, Fuegia Basket, and two men, York Minster and Jemmy Button, as they were 'named'. On a previous voyage the captain had taken them hostage in reprisal for the theft of the ship's whaler. He then had the crazy notion of carting them off to England, giving them a crash-course in Christianity and returning them to their native land to help spread the gospel. Now (having been presented to William IV and Queen Adelaide), they were on their way home in the *Beagle*, accompanied by an English clergyman, the Reverend Richard Matthews, and bearing an incredible range of items including wineglasses, soup-tureens and tea-trays, all presumably intended as tokens of the faith. The experiment was a sordid failure. The parson lost all his equipment within a matter of days, and Jemmy Button ended up leading a massacre of foreign sailors.

Slavery – only abolished in the West Indies in 1833 and not until 1863 in the United States – was another abrasive issue. Captain Fitzroy, fervent Christian though he was (but then it was always the most pious who had made a fat profit out of their commerce in fellow-humans), fiercely supported the practice. Darwin, in-

Wigwam Cove took its name 'from some of the Fuegian habitations; but every bay in the neighbourhood might be so called. The inhabitants, living chiefly upon shell-fish, are obliged constantly to change their place of residence'. Huge piles of old shells marked their presence.

fluenced by Uncle Jos, who played such a prominent role in the anti-slavery campaign, was equally opposed to the barbarous system. In Brazil, incidentally, he thought far more highly of the Negro slaves than of the Brazilians themselves 'who are as contemptible in their minds as their persons are miserable'. He only hoped that the day would come when the slaves would assert their own rights, but forget to avenge their wrongs.

For Darwin, the first few weeks of the voyage were wretched for reasons unconnected with the tantrums of Captain Fitzroy. He was laid low by seasickness and rightly remarked that 'the misery is excessive and far exceeds what a person would suppose who had never been at sea more than a few days'. However, Darwin was far too enthralled by all that went on to be discountenanced unduly by an ailment which, after all, Nelson and many a professional sailor had endured. One ostensibly insignificant incident shows the ferment that was already beginning to stir in his mind. When the *Beagle* was south of the Canaries, he started trawling, with an improvised bag made of bunting attached to a semicircular bow, for marine creatures – plankton, in other words, though he did not use the term. Many of these tiny creatures, he said, were so low in the scale of nature, yet so exquisite in their forms and rich colours, that it was a cause of wonder that so much beauty should apparently be created for such little purpose. It is clear that Darwin, albeit subconsciously at the time, thought there *must* be some purpose in their existence.

Again, on the island of St Jago, in the Cape Verde group which he was particularly interested to visit because of Humboldt's description,

I returned to the shore, treading on volcanic rocks, hearing the notes of unknown birds and seeing new insects fluttering about still newer flowers. It has been for me a glorious day, like giving to a blind man eyes, he is overwhelmed with what he sees and cannot easily comprehend it. Such are my feelings and such may they remain.

To appreciate what all this signified, it is essential constantly to bear in mind that Captain Fitzroy was no crank in the eyes of the vast majority of his contemporaries. 'The Book! The Book!' – Fitzroy's war-cry – was all that mattered. It should be added here that in spite of all their growing fundamental differences, Fitzroy developed almost a fondness for his young companion. He wrote to Captain Francis Beaufort, the Admiralty hydrographer who had instigated the voyage, that 'Darwin is a very sensible, hard-working man, and a very pleasant mess-mate. I never saw a "shore-going fellow" come into the ways of a ship so soon and so thoroughly as Darwin'. And later, 'Darwin is a regular trump!'

Perhaps the captain was affected by Darwin's single-minded enthusiasm which shows through vividly all the time, as for example when he first set foot in South America.

I have been wandering by myself in a Brazilian forest: amongst the multitude it is hard to say what set of objects is most striking; the general luxuriance of the vegetation bears the victory, the elegance of the grasses, the novelty of the parasitical plants, the beauty of the flowers, the glossy green of the foliage, all tends to this end. A most paradoxical mixture of sound and silence pervades the shady parts of the wood: the noise from the insects is so loud that in the evening it can be heard even in a vessel anchored several hundred yards from the shore: yet within the recesses of the forest a universal stillness appears to reign.

Now of course the purpose of Darwin's voyage was scientific. Everybody knows the profound effects it was to have on his own thinking and that of the entire civilized world. But there is one aspect of the book directly arising from the *Beagle* expedition that is usually neglected. Many people imagine Darwin to have been extraordinarily learned and, *ipso facto*, extraordinarily dull. Perhaps they are daunted by the title of his *Journal of Researches into the Natural History and Geology of the Countries Visited during the Voyage round the World of H.M.S. Beagle*. Yet in fact is is one of the best travel books ever written. It has been paraphrased or adapted a score of times, but it needs no softening hand to make it readable. Joseph Dalton Hooker sums it up when he quotes a letter from the second master of the *Terror* (sister ship of the *Erebus* on Ross's Antarctic voyage): 'I like Darwin's Journal much: he has accomplished what old Johnson said of Goldsmith when he heard he was going to write a Natural History: "He will make it as interesting as a Persian tale".'

Because of his own enthusiasm and sincerity, together with his lucid style, Darwin is invariably entertaining, even when, for example, he is describing an apparently unpromising subject such as the diodon or globe-fish, alias sea hedgehog. This fish has the power of distending the oesophagus or gullet with air, so that the body becomes blown out like a balloon. The skin is covered with spines, and these, on the inflation of the body, become a highly effective defence. Darwin was intrigued by the frequent cases of diodon being found 'floating, alive and distended, in the stomach of a shark; on several occasions it has been known to eat its way not only through the coats of the stomach, but through the sides of the monster, which has thus been killed. Who would ever have imagined that a little soft fish could have destroyed the great and savage shark'.

Going to another extreme, Darwin holds our attention when discussing an even more unpromising subject – that of fossils. He made extremely important discoveries of these near Bahia Blanca in Brazil, starting with the unearthing of the head of a megatherium, an immense extinct relation of the giant sloth.

The great size of the bones of the Megatheroid animals, including the Megatherium, Megalonyx, Scelidotherium, and Mylodon, is truly wonderful. The habits of life of these animals were a complete puzzle to naturalists, until Professor Owen★ solved the problem with remarkable ingenuity. The teeth indicate, by their simple structure, that these Megatheroid animals lived on vegetable food, and probably on the leaves and small twigs of trees; their ponderous forms and great strong curved claws seem so little adapted for locomotion, that some eminent naturalists have actually believed that, like the sloths, to which they are intimately related, they subsisted by climbing back downwards on trees, and feeding on the leaves. It was a bold, not to say preposterous idea to conceive even antediluvian trees with branches strong enough to bear animals as large as elephants. Professor Owen, with far more probability, believes that, instead of climbing on the trees, they pulled the branches down to them, and tore up the smaller ones by the roots, and so fed on the leaves. The colossal breadth and weight of their hinder quarters, which can hardly be imagined without having been seen, become, on this view, of obvious service, instead of being an encumbrance: their apparent clumsiness disappears. With their great tails and their huge heels firmly fixed like a tripod on the ground, they could freely exert the full force of their most powerful arms and great claws. Strongly rooted, indeed, must that tree have been, which could have resisted such a force! The Mylodon, moreover, was furnished with a long extensile tongue like that of the giraffe, which, by one of those beautiful provisions of nature, thus reaches with the aid of its long neck its leafy food. I may remark, that in Abyssinia, the elephant, when it cannot reach with its proboscis the branches, deeply scores with its tusks the trunk of the tree, up and down and all round, till it is sufficiently weakened to be broken down.

Geology was for long Darwin's prime interest and in this connection he had the good fortune, paradoxical though that may sound, of being present at what, up to the time, was considered to be the worst earthquake ever to occur in Chile. He was so horrified by the damage and distress that he went on to outline what could have been the basis of a twentieth-century science-fiction story.

Earthquakes alone are sufficient to destroy the prosperity of any country. If beneath England the now inert subterranean forces should exert those powers which most assuredly in former geological ages they have exerted, how completely would the entire condition of the country be changed! What would become of the lofty houses, thickly packed cities, great manufactories, the beautiful public and private edifices? If the new period of disturbance were first to commence by some great earthquake in the dead of night, how terrific would be the carnage! England would at once be bankrupt; all papers, records, and accounts would from that moment be lost. Government being unable to collect the taxes, and failing to maintain its authority, the hand of violence and rapine would remain uncontrolled. In every large town famine would go forth, pestilence and death following in its train.

But Darwin the geologist was able to draw vital deductions from such disasters in South America.

I have convincing proof that this part of the continent has been elevated near the coast at least 400 to 500, and in some parts from 1,000 to 1,300 feet, since the epoch of existing shells; and further inland the rise may have been greater.

From all this he began to realize the falsity of Cuvier's theories about the Creation (which will be mentioned in the next chapter). For it was becoming evident to Darwin from the geological phenomena he encountered that a continual evolution of the earth itself had taken place.

Crammed though the *Journal of Researches* necessarily is with scientific material, it is rich also in subjects totally unrelated to Darwin's essential researches, from his colourful adventures with the gauchos of the Argentine to the funeral customs of the Maoris of New Zealand. He is unfailingly readable and, as the great Humboldt complained, the book was not sufficiently widely read in England 'because the author is a zoologist, which you imagine to be synonymous with bore'.

★Sir Richard Owen helped Darwin with the classification and arrangement of his *Beagle* collection and contributed to the *Zoology of the Voyage of the Beagle* (1840). John Gould wrote and illustrated the section on birds, Thomas Bell wrote up the reptiles and Leonard Jenyns the fishes.

16 Confessing a Murder

Nowadays, when evolution is taken for granted, it needs an effort of the imagination to appreciate that little more than a hundred years ago the great majority of people, including some of the most respected intellects of the period, still firmly believed in the idea of the Creation as described in the Book of Genesis.

One such theory still current at the time of Darwin's voyage in the *Beagle* had been propounded by Baron Cuvier (who only died when Darwin was in the middle of his expedition). A factor that had always disturbed the fundamentalists, led by Cuvier, who was himself a stern Lutheran, just as Linnaeus had been, was the existence of fossils, especially as they seemed to follow progressive sequences. Cuvier explained away this awkward hint of evolution by declaring that at various times a series of catastrophes had completely destroyed entire animal and plant populations. It was from such cosmic upheavals, reruns of 'darkness upon the face of the deep', that the offending fossils had resulted. Subsequently the Almighty reflected on his original handiwork and went back to the drawing-board, as it were. He then proceeded to repopulate the earth with a brand-new collection of improved species.

The patronage Cuvier had enjoyed ended with the French Revolution. He was obliged to take a job as tutor to a wealthy family at Caen. Here he was able to spend much time on the Normandy coast studying marine life and planning his reclassification of the animal kingdom.

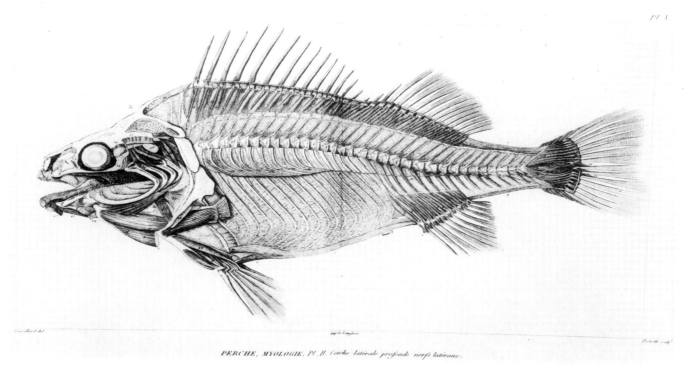

PERCHE, MYOLOGIE, Pl. II. Couche latérale profonde nerfs latéraux.

Darwin wrote about the Galapagos tortoise: 'Near the springs it was a curious spectacle to behold many of these huge creatures, one set eagerly travelling onwards with outstretched necks, and another set returning, after having drunk their fill. When the tortoise arrives at the spring, quite regardless of any spectator, he buries his head in the water above his eyes, and greedily swallows great mouthfuls, at the rate of ten in a minute.'

Much as Darwin himself had believed in the literal truth of the Bible, doubts, uncomfortable though they were, mounted steadily in his mind. Greatly influenced by *The Principles of Geology* (1830–3) by Sir Charles Lyell, to whom he said he could never sufficiently express his debt, Darwin began to detect evidence that this 'catastrophe' notion simply could not be accepted. One such occasion was when, thanks to his never-failing powers of observation, he saw that the fossilized bones of the extinct giant sloth, which he excavated in Patagonia, were embedded in types of marine shells that still existed. This could only mean that Baron Cuvier's catastrophes had not resulted in everything being swept away in one fell swoop, such as a Noah-type flood.

If the *Beagle* in general laid the foundations for so much of what was to be his principal work, it was the

(Opposite) The Galapagos iguana is now on the danger list. The settlers' cats kill it, their pigs eat the eggs, and it has been slain for its skin. Full grown it reaches three feet or more in length.

Galapagos Islands which provided the biggest clue in his theory of evolution. It was here on the equator that he really began to see that natural species could not possibly have been created in an unchanging, once-and-for-all form. More than any other discovery during his voyage, the Galapagos started him on the trail that eventually led to the *Origin of Species*.

Five or six hundred miles out in the Pacific from Ecuador, the archipelago is volcanic in origin, having been thrown up by underwater disturbances during the later Tertiary Era. But it is probable that the colonization of the islands by flora and fauna from the South American mainland took place only just before Pleistocene times; that is, in the last million years. The Galapagos take their name from the Spanish word for the giant tortoise, for which they are famous – though, owing to relentless slaughter in the past, it is now an endangered species. The islands were discovered in 1535 by Fray Tomas de Berlanga, Bishop of Panama in the days of the Spanish conquistadores, but were not inhabited by human beings until shortly before the visit of the *Beagle*. Through the centuries, however, they were regularly visited by buccaneers, whalers and sealers in quest of freshwater and meat – in the form of the tortoises, some of which can weigh up to five hundred pounds. It is reckoned that in little more than thirty years in the last century over fifteen thousand giant tortoises were slaughtered. Though this creature is a land species, it is known that its ancestor could have arrived from the mainland, for some land tortoises are perfectly capable of surviving in sea-water for a considerable time.

Darwin was immediately intrigued by the way the Spaniards were able to identify the particular island from which a particular species of tortoise had come. In the same way he found that there were various types of mocking-bird on different islands. Most striking of all was the case of the Galapagos 'finches', or *geospizi*, which are peculiar to the islands.

The most curious fact is the perfect gradation in the size of the beaks in the different species, from one as large as that of a hawfinch to that of a chaffinch. Seeing this gradation and diversity of structure in one small, intimately related group of birds, one might really fancy that from an original paucity of

birds in this archipelago one species had been taken and modified for different ends.

Each individual island was inhabited by a different species of the same genus of 'finch', coming from a common ancestor, probably part of the American buntings' subfamily, the *emberizinae*. In addition, on individual islands distinct species had exploited what in modern terminology would be called different biological niches. Some of the birds had gradually become adapted to insect feeding; others had developed more powerful beaks for seed-eating; others had parrot-like beaks; another variety had straight wood-boring beaks. But virtually the only difference between these varieties of birds was in the shape of their beaks.

Darwin was being drawn to the conclusion that everything he had gleaned on the Galapagos implied a rapid process of evolution. Yet in spite of this startling evidence, it was not on this that he set to work when at last he arrived home in 1836. To begin with he concentrated on his book of the voyage, the *Journal of Researches*. With Gilbert White as his example, he was always a meticulous note-taker and, thanks to this, he finished the book, not far short of a quarter of a million words in length, in six months. His original field notebooks, bound in red leather, can still be seen at Down House in Kent where he settled in 1839 and spent the rest of his life.

It is interesting to note that the original sub-title of the *Journal* stated that the researches were into geology and natural history. This order of priorities was not reversed until the second edition appeared in 1845. Geology was still Darwin's first preoccupation. He now embarked on a trio of important books on the subject: *The Structure and Distribution of Coral Reefs* (1842), *Geological Observations on Volcanic Islands* (1844) and *Geological Observations on South America* (1846). He was also for three years Secretary of the Geological Society.

Following these weighty but important tomes, he threw himself into an eight-year study of barnacles. As he explains in his autobiography, he became interested in them in Chile because of a curious burrowing barnacle

PTEROGLOSSUS DERBIANUS.
Derby's Groove-bill Aracari.

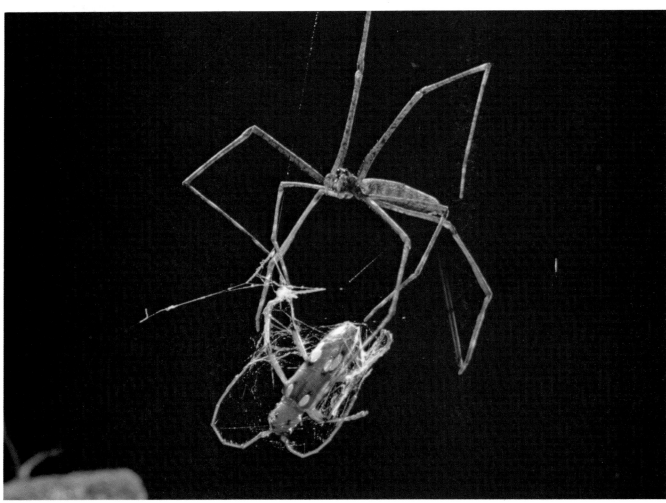

so different from other species that a new sub-order had to be made to accommodate them. Down House became so taken over by Darwin's 'beloved barnacles' that when one of his small sons (he had married his cousin Emma Wedgwood in 1838) went to tea with some young friends he solemnly asked them when *their* father 'did his barnacles'.

It is strange that Darwin should have been so many years coming into the open with his theory of evolution. In contrast with the energetic young man who had endured so much physical hardship during the voyage with the *Beagle* – mountainous seas, cramped quarters, journeys on horseback of hundreds of miles across the pampas, mountain climbing – Darwin subsequently never enjoyed good health. It has been suggested, though not proved, that while in the tropics he might have contracted Chagas's disease, carried by a 'most disgusting' blood-sucking bug. Whatever its cause, ill-health did not impair his output, and the delay in the expounding of his theory seems to have derived largely from more personal concerns. Darwin's father was bitterly opposed to the notion of evolution and Emma was positively shocked by such a denial of the orthodox version of the Creation. Darwin himself, as has been mentioned, started off as a true believer and, being well aware of how his 'blasphemy' would be greeted, seems to have been anxious to put off the day of revelation.

Even when, tentatively, he began to come out with it, he was extremely apologetic. 'At last gleams of light have come,' he wrote to his close friend Joseph Dalton Hooker in 1844, 'and I am almost convinced (quite contrary to the opinion I started with) that species are not (it is like confessing a murder) immutable. I think I have found out (here's presumption!) the simplest way by which species become exquisitely adapted to various ends. You will groan and think to yourself, "on what a man have I been wasting my time and writing to". I should five years ago have thought so.'

In addition to his findings on the *Beagle* voyage, Darwin amassed an immense amount of material on the subject of evolution by natural selection. He even consulted pigeon fanciers, from whom he learned that by breeding from selected varieties, it was possible to obtain new kinds of pigeon. In his own Kentish garden he kept a small plot of ground in which he purposely let the weeds flourish. Every springtime he carefully marked each weed as it appeared. He recorded that at one point 350 plants had come up, but that almost at once two-thirds of them had been eaten by slugs. Why, he wondered, had the others survived?

At the back of his mind all this time was a book that had great influence on his thinking. This was *An Essay on the Principle of Population* (1798) by Thomas Robert Malthus. This clergyman-cum-economist had warned that if Man's inherent urge to reproduce was not kept in check by natural counterbalances, over-population would result and a struggle for existence would ensue. The struggle for existence! Darwin realized that it was only the fittest that would survive such a struggle. This was how evolution had come about, through natural selection, the weaker animals or plants going to the wall, the stronger surviving and improving. The idea came suddenly to Darwin one day when he was out driving through the countryside. Snap!

This was the cue for Alfred Russel Wallace to make his entry on the scene. When Darwin returned from his adventures, Wallace was still a boy of thirteen. Because of various paternal mishaps in financial matters, much of Wallace's childhood was spent in a cottage on the banks of the River Usk in Wales, where fishermen still used wickerwork coracles. It was here that his interest in nature started, chiefly through catching lampreys. But because of family circumstances, he was forced to take a job when he was fourteen, and there was no hope of his going to university. So under the instruction of his brother William, he started training as a land-surveyor, as this did not require a degree. But William died suddenly as a result of sleeping in a damp bed after catching cold in 'a wretched open third class carriage', a sadly ironical death for one whose work was essential for the railways that were snaking out across the land.

However, Wallace continued in his job and, as it literally took him across country all the time, it afforded him many opportunities for nature study. Then, while working in Leicestershire, he had one of those formative encounters that often take place. In a local library he met Henry Walter Bates, 'an enthusiastic entomologist whose speciality was beetle collecting, though he also had a good set of British butterflies'. Bates was indeed 'an enthusiastic entomologist' and became famous for his work on mimicry among insects, an important aspect of the law of natural selection. He was to open up a new and wonderful prospect for Wallace.

He asked me to see his collection, and I was amazed to find the great number and variety of beetles, their many strange forms and often beautiful markings or colouring, and was even more surprised when I found that almost all had been collected around Leicester, and that there were still many more to be discovered. If I had been asked before how many kinds of beetles were to be found in any small district near a town, I should probably have guessed about fifty or at the outside a hundred, and thought that a very liberal allowance. But I now heard that there were probably a thousand different kinds within ten miles of the town.

For the time being Wallace continued his job of surveying for the new railways. But he became pro-

In spite of the coincidence of their scientific findings, Wallace (opposite) and Darwin were very different in character. When Darwin encountered the natives of Tierra del Fuego, he was revolted by them. Wallace could write of Amazonian Indians (below): 'The most unexpected sensation of surprise and delight was my first meeting and living with a man in a state of nature – with absolutely uncontaminated savages. They were all going about their own work or pleasure which had nothing to do with the white men or their ways; they walked with the free step of the independent forest dweller – and in every detail they were original and self-sustaining, as are the wild animals of the forest.'

Mary Kingsley (niece of Charles Kingsley). Her *Travels in West Africa* (1897) caused an immediate sensation, her journeys being an astonishing feat for a woman in the days when Queen Victoria was celebrating her diamond jubilee.

gressively dissatisfied by this, partly because of the manoeuvrings of the 'robber railway barons' and partly because he had, as one might say, been bitten by the collecting bug. At the age of twenty-five he turned professional naturalist.

This in other words meant a collector for museums, a profession which expanded throughout the nineteenth century – the intrepid explorer Mary Kingsley went out to West Africa in the 1890s collecting tropical fish for the British Museum. The two friends now conceived an adventurous plan to journey along the River Amazon, which in those days was still very much a river of danger, awe and mystery. Bates leaves a portrait, caricature almost, of the collector at work, perhaps surprising to a later generation who no longer even collect birds' eggs and prefer to see their nature wild, or recorded for them on film, rather than as stuffed specimens.

Between nine and ten a.m. I prepare for the woods; a coloured shirt, pair of trousers, pair of common boots, and an old felt hat are all my clothing; over my left shoulder slings my double-barrelled gun, loaded one with No. 10, one with No. 4 shot. In my right hand I take my net; on my left side is suspended a leathern bag with two pockets, one for my insect-box, the other for powder and two kinds of shot; on my right side hangs my 'game-bag', an ornamental affair, with red leather trappings and thongs to hang lizards, snakes, frogs, or large birds. One small pocket in this bag contains my caps; another, papers for wrapping up delicate birds; others for wads, cotton, box of powdered plaster; and a box with damped cork for the Micro-Lepidoptera; to my shirt is pinned my pin-cushion, with six sizes of pins.

Bates was to remain in South America for eleven years; Wallace for four years. But long before that he had parted company with Bates, wishing to make a solo expedition along the Rio Negro. While he was in the Amazon basin he gathered an immense collection, but was destined to lose every scrap of it. Three weeks after he set sail for home, in 1852, his ship caught fire.

I went down into the cabin, now suffocatingly hot and full of smoke, to see what was worth saving. I got my watch and a small tin box containing some shirts and a couple of old notebooks, with some drawings of plants and animals, and scrambled up with them on deck. Many clothes and a large portfolio of drawings and sketches remained in my berth; but I did not care to venture down again, and in fact felt a kind of apathy about saving anything that I can now hardly account for. The Captain at length ordered all into the boats, and was himself the last to leave the vessel.

With what pleasure had I looked upon every rare and curious insect I had added to my collection! How many times, when almost overcome by ague, had I crawled into the forest and been rewarded by some unknown and beautiful species! How many places,

which no European foot but my own had trodden, would have been recalled to my memory by the rare birds and insects they had furnished to my collection!

And now everything was gone, and I had not one specimen to illustrate the unknown lands I had trod or to call back the recollection of the wild scenes I had beheld! But such regrets I knew were vain, and I tried to think as little as possible about what might have been and to occupy myself with the state of things which actually existed.

Wallace came home with a growing restlessness of mind about the origin of all the stunningly brilliant life he had seen in these mysterious forests into which he had ventured. Resolutely he went off for eight years' collecting in the Far East. It was now that one of the strangest scientific coincidences was to take place. In the Moluccas, while he was suffering from a bout of fever, he happened to remember the selfsame book by Malthus that had such an influence on Darwin. Wallace was struck by the same intellectual flash that Darwin had experienced.

It occurred to me to ask the question, Why do some die and some live? And the answer was clearly, that on the whole the best fitted live. From the effects of disease the most healthy escaped; from enemies, the strongest, the swiftest, or the most cunning; from famine, the best hunters or those with the best digestion; and so on.

Then I at once saw, that the ever present variability of all living things would furnish the material from which, by the mere weeding out of those less adapted to the actual conditions, the fittest alone would continue the race.

There suddenly flashed upon me the idea of the survival of the fittest.

The more I thought over it, the more I became convinced that I had at length found the long-sought-for law of nature that solved the problem of the Origin of Species. I waited anxiously for the termination of my fit so that I might at once make notes for a paper on the subject. The same evening I did this pretty fully, and on two succeeding evenings wrote it out carefully in order to send it to Darwin by the next post, which would leave in a day or two.

Wallace marvelled at the rich magnificence of plant life in the valley of the Amazon. With the 'exception of some very small portions' it was completely covered with primeval forest and he wished he could have travelled over it in a balloon. Nowadays those 'very small portions' are far bigger and the noise of the bulldozer is heard in the land.

Though Wallace, as he said, knew that Darwin was interested in the subject, he had no idea how much Darwin had worked on and agonized over it all. Wallace's 'paper' must have come as a staggering blow when it arrived at Down House. For twenty years Darwin had wrestled with 'his' theory and his own misgivings and now as he said, 'I never saw a more striking coincidence; if Wallace had my MS sketch written out in 1842, he could not have made a better short abstract! Even his terms now stand as heads of my chapters. . . . So all my originality, whatever it may amount to, will be smashed. . . .'

Darwin might well have paid dearly for his procrastination and diffidence. The immediate dilemma was resolved by his friends Hooker and Lyell, on whom he always relied so much. Rather than let him sink without trace, they arranged to read a paper on the Origin of Species by each of the protagonists at a meeting of the Linnean Society in 1858. This was done and went off without any stir. But now Darwin simply had to go ahead with writing the book itself – 'the accursed Book', as he called it. But by now he had a clear field. Wallace, a big man in every way – he was over six feet tall – stood aside and allowed Darwin not only the use of all his findings but all the credit as well. Darwin referred to his noble generosity.

An indication of the turmoil to come can be seen in the reaction of John Murray, who had published the *Journal of Researches* with such success in 1839. On the recommendation of Sir Charles Lyell, Murray committed himself to publishing the *Origin of Species* without seeing it beforehand. 'I have no hesitation in swerving from my usual routine and in stating at once, even without seeing the MS, that I shall be most happy to publish it on my usual terms.' A sentiment to gladden the heart of any author.

But when Mr Murray did start reading the piecemeal manuscript, he had distinct qualms. He doubted the scientific credibility of such a book. An edition of five hundred copies was all he deemed practicable. Fortunately he was persuaded otherwise. *On the Origin of Species by Means of Natural Selection* was published on 24 November 1859, price fifteen shillings. Booksellers bought up the entire edition on the same day. Less than two months later a second edition had a similar success.

Witnessing an earthquake at Valdivia in Chile, Darwin had written: 'A bad earthquake at once destroys our old associations: the earth, the very emblem of solidity, has moved beneath our feet like a thin crust over a fluid.' Little did he anticipate how aptly his words could in time have been applied to the effect of his revolutionary book. There was a rustle of Victorian hands being raised in horror. Even Adam Sedgwick, his original professor of geology, was aghast and said he had read the book with more pain than pleasure. 'I call causation the will of God; and I can prove that He acts for the good of His creatures.' The most vicious attack, in the form of an anonymous critique in the *Edinburgh Review*, came from another professor, Sir Richard Owen, who had been so close to Darwin at one time that he had actually helped with the organization of his vast *Beagle* collection. The Church, typified by Bishop Wilberforce (nicknamed Soapy Sam), was especially outraged. One eminent clergyman denounced Darwin as the most dangerous man in England.

But if the Church was scandalized because Darwin was sapping at its very foundations, there were other men who in effect cried, 'Well said old mole! canst work i'th'earth so fast? A worthy pioneer!' For assuredly Darwin did not lack champions. Even some broader-minded churchmen, such as Charles Kingsley and Cannon Tristram, zoologist of the Bible, supported him. There was Wallace, of course, and Bates, as well as botanists such as Hooker, Lyell, the greatest geologist of his day, Sir John Lubbock, the naturalist, and the philosopher Herbert Spencer. But undoubtedly Darwin's most effective champion was T.H. Huxley, the most brilliant zoologist in England, who earned the nickname of 'Darwin's bulldog'. And the ultimate accolade came when Karl Marx asked permission to dedicate *Das Kapital* to Darwin, who modestly refused the honour.

To a later age, the theory of evolution, the struggle for existence, the survival of the fittest (whatever its unfortunate connotations), seem so logical, that sometimes one is left wondering what all the fuss was about.

Pigeon fanciers existed long before Darwin's time. According to Pliny, the Romans had a craze for pigeons. They built special closed towers in which they fattened them for the table. But the Egyptians were more advanced: they used pigeons to fly out north, south, east and west to announce the coronation of Rameses II in 1204 B.C.

17 The Brilliant Fundamentalist

'Coolly bowing aside God's authority, this writer has hatched a scheme, by which the immediate ancestor of Adam was a Chimpanzee, and his remote ancestor a Maggot!'

Not, as might be supposed, Bishop Wilberforce railing against the author of the *Origin of Species*, but one of Darwin's fellow-naturalists, Philip Henry Gosse. Perhaps more than anyone, he represents the genuine distress caused by the theory of evolution that was going the rounds. For Gosse's words were published in 1857, a couple of years before the actual appearance of Darwin's book, though as an associate member of the Linnean Society he might have heard, or heard of, the original papers of Darwin and Wallace.

Gosse was not even satisfied by the beliefs of Cuvier and his followers that the six 'days' of the Inspired Record, as he termed it, signified six successive periods of immense though undefined duration. Who would dare suggest as absurd, Gosse protested, the idea 'that the strata of the surface of the earth, with their fossil floras and faunas, may possibly belong to a prochronic development of the mighty plan of the life-history of this world?'

In plainer language, he was suggesting that the earth was created with fossil skeletons already in its crust.

It may be objected that, to assume the world to have been created with fossil skeletons in its crust – skeletons of animals that never really existed – is to charge the Creator with forming objects whose sole purpose was to deceive us. The reply is obvious. Were the concentric timber-rings of a created tree formed merely to deceive? Were the growth lines of a created shell intended to deceive? Was the navel of the created Man intended to deceive him into the persuasion that he had had a parent?

Even if they did not express themselves in such metaphysical terms, there were many scientists of the period who found it agonizingly difficult to reconcile the strong case for the theory of evolution with their religious beliefs. Gosse was an extreme case, as is shown by the passage above from *Omphalos: An Attempt to Untie the Geological Knot*. Rather than untying the knot, Gosse succeeded only in tying himself in knots. At least Gosse

Wallace wrote that if his family circumstances had been more affluent he would not have taken up collecting and gone to the Amazon. Likewise, the boyhood of Philip Henry Gosse was passed in straitened circumstances and he was forced to take a job that sent him abroad – to the ultimate great benefit of natural history.

came out with it openly. But it all earned him a good deal of ridicule from his contemporaries. The unkindest cut of all came from his close friend Charles Kingsley, himself a pillar of the Church. In the fourth, 1859 edition of his *Glaucus*, Kingsley said: 'It is with real pain that I have seen my friend Mr Gosse, since this book was first written, make a step in the direction of obscurantism, which I can only call desperate, by publishing a book called *Omphalos*.'

This aberration aside, Gosse was one of the finest naturalists of the nineteenth century and his *British Sea-Anemones and Corals* is still a classic today. Born in 1810, just a year after Charles Darwin, Gosse parted company with his fellows because of his fanatical religious views. But, though Darwin has had such a profound effect on our thinking, it is possible that, by his many brilliant and readable books, Gosse was closer to ordinary people who were being drawn in their thousands to a study of nature. Fortunately for us Gosse had a devoted and objective biographer in his son, the late Sir Edmund Gosse, with his *Life of Philip Gosse* (1890); while his *Father and Son* (1907) is a most witty and perceptive 'Study of Two Temperaments', as it is sub-titled.

Gosse had a far more frugal upbringing than did Darwin. His father was a miniaturist, and though he earned only a pittance from this work, he did at least pass on to Gosse his skill in drawing and in the use of colours. Gosse's books, especially those about the sea-shore, were to be illustrated by his own detailed pictures, in which his draughtsmanship served him well. As for his early interest in nature, he had to thank an aunt who encouraged him to keep sea anemones in jugs of sea-water. (Wallace as a small boy had scooped up lampreys from the River Usk with a rusty saucepan.)

There was no university for Gosse. He did not even finish school. His parents were so poorly off they were forced to take him away from his school at Blandford in Dorset when he was fifteen. However, he had at least learned some basic Greek and Latin there, which were to be invaluable to him as a professional naturalist later. He was fortunate in the job he took, that of a clerk in a firm of ship's chandlers in Poole, where he worked for two years. Then, in 1827, his employers sent him out to Carbonear in Newfoundland, where he stayed for seven years.

This was the turning-point of his life, for his work brought him in contact with fishermen and sealers. He saw their catches, heard their stories, witnessed their wrecks. He started to keep a nature journal and, just as Humboldt's *Personal Narrative* had set Darwin on his path, a book called *Essays on the Microscope* aroused Gosse's enthusiasm. He began avidly to study insects and even kept jars of them on his desk so that he could keep an eye on them while he totted up accounts.

His resourcefulness is shown by the fact that when he went back to England for a visit, he bought two microscope lenses, mounted them in bone, and, he records, used an old toothbrush handle for a focusing scale. This in itself is eloquent. In these days of lavish research facilities, it is difficult to appreciate the handicaps under which men such as Gosse had to work.

After seven years in Newfoundland, Gosse decided to broaden his experience. He launched out into farming in Canada, and though his three-year efforts were a failure as far as agriculture was concerned, they undoubtedly enriched his knowledge of nature, even to the extent of being squirted over by a skunk. Shaking the dust or

Gosse could be equally vivid with his illustrations as with his written descriptions. Fabre, his contemporary, had to wait for illustrations to his books until his son Paul took up photography.

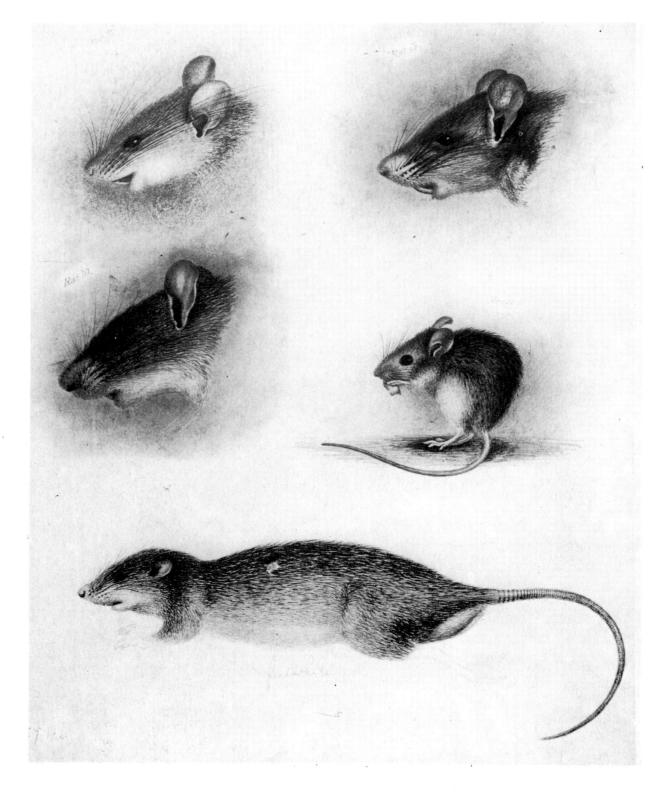

The chameleon moves more slowly than any other reptile. Its speed is in its club-shaped tongue. Moving within range of an insect, it opens its mouth hesitantly, like a cautious speaker, then shoots out its tongue to almost the length of its body and deftly catches its victim on the sticky tip.

rather the snow of Canada from his feet, he next landed up in Alabama. Here, shades of Audubon, he was obliged to take a job teaching in a village school. But while he was there he spent his spare time pursuing his insect studies. He gathered enough material for a book on insects and made nearly 250 detailed illustrations in colour for it. That book was never published; however, in the meantime he was also at work on *The Canadian Naturalist*, and when he returned to England in 1839 this was accepted for publication.

Modest though his success with this book was, it came just in time. So hard up was he, that, to his chagrin, he had been forced to sell the collection of bird skins he had made during his sojourn in North America. He records that on his return to London he could usually only afford food such as cheap herring, and even then he had to discipline himself to chew it as slowly as possible in order to eke it out.

Philip Gosse, as will have been gathered, had had no training whatsoever as a naturalist. He was entirely self-taught. There was now no other course for him than to become a professional, and with this in mind he worked

day after day in the Natural History Department of the British Museum. He succeeded so well at his do-it-yourself zoological course that the Museum employed him as a collector and sent him out to Jamaica. Collecting was then at its height and though, undoubtedly, collectors plundered nature right and left, it was all in the interests of science and they added immeasurably to people's knowledge of the 'wonders and prodigies of Nature'.

If I rode with vasculum and insect-net and fowling-piece into the mountain woods, there was still the pleasing uncertainty of what might occur, with the certainty of abundance. A fine epiphyte orchid scents the air with fragrance, and it is discovered far up in the fork of some vast tree; then there is the palpitation of hope and fear as we discuss the possibility of getting it down; then come contrivances and efforts – pole after pole is cut and tied together with the cords which the forest creepers afford. At length the plant is reached, and pushed off, and triumphantly bagged. But lo! while examining it, some elegant twisted shell is dis-

(Opposite) Gosse always laid it down that the natural history of animals should inform us of 'their sayings and doings and if we have their portraits, let us have them drawn from life, while their bright eyes are glancing'. The naturalist must study nature live and close by. The laboratory was essential for some aspects of natural history, but it could not replace field-work.

covered, with its tenant snail, crawling on the leaves.

Scarcely is this boxed, when a gorgeous butterfly rushes out of the gloom into the sunny glade, and is in a moment seen to be a novelty: then comes the excitement of pursuit; the disappointment of seeing it dance over a thicket out of sight; the joy of finding it reappear, the tantalizing trial of watching the lovely wings flapping just out of reach; the patient waiting for it to descend; the tiptoe approach as we see it settle on a flower; the breathless eagerness with which the net is poised; and the triumphant flush with which we contemplate the painted wings within the gauze; and the admiration with which we gaze on its loveliness when held in the trembling fingers.

Another step or two, and a gay-plumaged bird rises from the bush, and falls to the gun; we run to the spot and search for the game among the shrubs and moss; at last it is found, admired, and committed to a little protective cone of paper.

Birds of Jamaica established Gosse's reputation among his fellow-naturalists; while his complementary book, *A Naturalist's Sojourn in Jamaica*, gained him a considerable popular readership. When he returned to London he became increasingly immersed in his religious activities, parallel with his extremely arduous scientific work. He joined the Plymouth Brethren, preached to them and put his fundamentalist beliefs on paper. Added to this were family responsibilities, for he was now married and had a son. His extreme concentration on his work and the priority he accorded it are nicely caught in the oft-repeated quotation from his diary: 'E. delivered of a son. Received green swallow from Jamaica.'

But an even more delicious glimpse of this strange but brilliant man is given by Edmund Gosse in his *Father and Son*.

Another instance of the remarkable way in which the interests of daily life were mingled, in our strange household, with the practice of religion, made an impression upon my memory. We had all three been much excited by a report that a certain dark geometer-moth, generated in underground stables, had been met with in Islington. Its name, I think is, 'Boletobia fuliginaria', and I believe that it is ex-

tremely rare in England. We were sitting at family prayers on a summer morning, I think in 1855, when through the open window a brown moth came sailing. My Mother immediately interrupted the reading of the Bible by saying to my Father, 'O! Henry, do you think that can be "Boletobia"?' My Father rose up from the sacred book, examined the insect, which had now perched, and replied: 'No! it is only the common Vapourer, "Orgyia antiqua"!', resuming his seat, and the exposition of the Word, without any apology or embarrassment.

Not surprisingly, in view of all his religious concerns, together with his concentrated work at the microscope, Gosse had a breakdown. 'Bad case of nervous dyspepsia,' the doctor said. 'You must give up study, and go out of town.' It was a case of the ill-wind. Gosse and his family went off to live in Devon and it was here that he wrote some of his best work. He had already written an immensely successful book called *The Ocean*. Now he proceeded to write the classic *Sea-Anemones and Corals*, already mentioned, the very influential *The Aquarium* and the eminently readable and felicitous *A Naturalist's Rambles on the Devonshire Coast*.

Again, we are indebted to Edmund Gosse for some splendid glimpses of the naturalist at work.

The way in which my Father worked, in his most desperate escapades, was to wade breast-high into one of the huge pools, and examine the worm-eaten surface of the rock above and below the brim. In such remote places – spots where I could never venture, being left, a slightly timorous Andromeda, chained to a safer level of the cliff – in these extreme basins, there used often to lurk a marvellous profusion of animal and vegetable forms. My Father would search for the roughest and most corroded points of rock, those offering the best refuge for a variety of creatures, and would then chisel off fragments as low down in the water as he could. These pieces of rock were instantly plunged in the salt water of jars which we had brought with us for the purpose. When as much had been collected as we could carry away – my Father always dragged about an immense square basket, the creak of whose handles I can still fancy that I hear – we turned

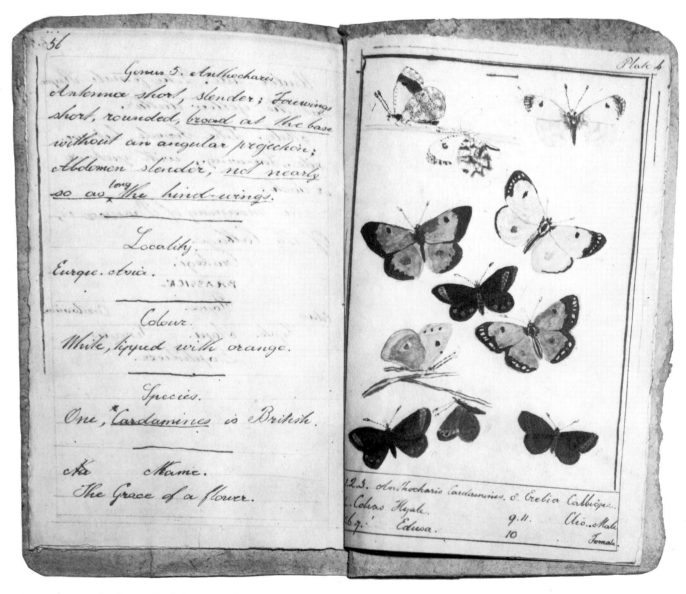

56

Genus 5. Anthocharis

Antennæ short, slender; forewings short, rounded, broad at the base without an angular projection; Abdomen slender, not nearly so as ~~long~~ the hind-wings.

Locality.

Europe. obvia.

Colour.

White, tipped with orange.

Species.

One, Cardamines is British.

Name.

The Grace of a flower.

1.2.3. Anthocharis Cardamines. & Erebia Cabbigea.
4. Colias Hyale.
5.6.7. Edusa.
8. 9.11. Clio. Male.
10. Female.

to trudge up the long climb home. Then all our prizes were spread out, face upward, in shallow pans of clean sea-water.

And, like a good horseman who, even after the toughest ride, will not see to his own comfort until his steed has been cared for, Gosse, still dripping wet from his sortie in the rock-pools, would immediately set to work on his marvellously accurate drawings to capture the brilliant colours of his prizes before they faded. But

Pages from one of the childhood notebooks of Edmund Gosse, who often helped his father. 'My eyes were extremely keen and powerful, though they were vexatiously near-sighted. Of no use in examining objects at any distance, in investigating a minute surface, my vision was trained to be invaluable.'

The old Fish House at Regent's Park, based on Gosse's work. After the First World War, the idea of an improved aquarium was revived. It incorporated the best features of aquaria all over the world and was opened in 1924 with E.C. Boulenger as its director. It cost £55,000, a large sum more than half a century ago, when a man was extremely well off with £1,000 a year, and was acknowledged to be the finest in the world.

superb though his illustrations were, particularly in *The Aquarium*, his written descriptions were always as exact and pellucid as the very water of those same rock-pools. He never fails to impart his own sense of wonder even when he is describing ostensibly unlikely subjects such as prawn or jellyfish or stone-boring mollusc or, as here, luminosity in some sea-tangle caused by polyps:

I had a frond of *Laminaria digitata*, on whose smooth surface a populous colony of that delicate zoophyte *Laemedea geniculata* had established itself. I had put the frond into a vessel of water as it came out of the sea, and the polypes were now in the highest health and vigour in a large vase in my study. After nightfall I went into the room, in the dark, and taking a slender stick struck the frond and waved it to and fro. Instantly one and another of the polypes lighted up, lamp after lamp rapidly seemed to catch the flame, until in a second or two every stalk bore several tiny but brilliant stars, while from the regular manner in which the stalks were disposed along the lines of the creeping stem, the spectacle bore a resemblance sufficiently striking to the illumination of a city; or rather to the gas-jets of some figure of a crown or V.R., adorning the house of a loyal citizen on a gala-night; the more because of the momentary extinction and relighting of the flames here and there, and the manner in which the successive ignition appeared to run rapidly from part to part.

During his studies of marine biology, Gosse made one discovery that was to have important effects. It was now realized that fish used up the oxygen in the water they inhabited, but replaced it with carbon dioxide. In contrast, aquatic plants absorbed carbon dioxide from the water to make starch by photosynthesis and replaced it with oxygen. This gave Gosse the idea that because of this symbiosis it should be possible to keep marine animals and aquatic plants alive together in a tank indefinitely. The waste product of one organism was vital supply to the other.

A chemist named Richard Warrington had already been making experiments in this connection a few years before and eventually succeeded in keeping goldfish and aquatic plants in company for several months. Gosse's experiments were carried out with rotifers, minute marine animals, and seaweed.

Should these experiments be perfected, what would hinder our keeping collections of marine animals for observation and study, even in London and other inland cities? Such a degree of success as I have attained would admit of so desirable a consummation, for even in London no great difficulty would be experienced in having a jar of sea-water brought up once in a couple of months. I hope to see the lovely marine Algae too, that hitherto have been almost unknown except pressed between the leaves of a book, growing in their native health and beauty, and waving their translucent fronds, on the tables of our drawing-rooms and on the shelves of our conservatories.

He got his wish. The 'Marine Aquarium for the Parlour or Conservatory' became immediately popular; indeed, it could be said that a craze for it set in. For Gosse's ideas came out at an auspicious time. A few years before, a penal tax on glass had been abolished – mainly through agitation on behalf of horticulturalists. In addition, all this time increasing numbers of people were becoming interested in nature study. Here was an opportunity of bringing some of the prodigies of nature into the home, as living illustrations to some of his books that were already there!

On a more important level, Gosse put his ideas to the Zoological Society of London. They were quick to appreciate the possibilities. With specimens from Gosse's own collection, they installed an experimental marine tank in the new Fish House at Regent's Park. This was so successful that in 1853 the Society opened the world's first 'marine aquavivarium'. Other aquaria followed in Britain and Europe. In 1884 the Marine Biological Association of Great Britain was founded. Its headquarters at Plymouth, Devon, with aquarium and laboratories, remains one of the leading marine stations in the world.

Although his ideas had in the meantime been greatly adapted and improved upon, it is to Gosse that must go much of the credit for marine biology being raised to the importance it now enjoys, with all its scientific and economic implications. And the enthusiast who proudly shows off his tropical fish in the comfort of his drawing-room can in part thank Philip Henry Gosse for being able to indulge his hobby.

18 Yearning for the Unknown

One of Gosse's less well-known books is *The Romance of Natural History*, of which there can have been but few editions since its original publication in 1860. Yet for his contemporary readers, who were without even the push-bike for personal travel, and for whom the chance of visiting exotic lands was infinitely remote, it must have seemed chockful of gripping material. One can envisage the pipe being puffed more tensely, or the quivering hand reaching for the bon-bon box, as the reader turned the pages.

In an age when there was no radio, no television, no easy travel facilities, no intimate, expert films to bring nature into people's homes, it was left to a writer such as Philip Gosse to meet the needs of a growingly inquisitive public. There was no lack of learned tomes, but people did not always want sedulous details about Lepidoptera or Coleoptera. Their curiosity, excitement even, had been aroused by men like Mungo Park, Banks, Parry, Waterton and Darwin. They were beginning to realize even in those, to us, halcyon days, how much they were cut off from nature.

Gosse aimed, he said, to present natural history in the individual way of a poet. He was concerned, not with mere statistics, but with the aesthetic aspect, with the human emotions – wonder, terror, revulsion, desire, and so forth – which are stimulated by contemplation of wildlife. He wrote in an age when the gorilla had just been 'introduced' to Western society, in the context of which his book was a considerable feat of popularization. Drawing on his own experiences and those of others, he vivifies the spectacle of nature in some of its many facets, conveying the emotions it generates: from the magic of the 'silver thaw' in Newfoundland when freezing rain turns the forest into a fairyland of tinkling, sparkling glass, to a hyena skulking away from some desert tomb with a human skull in its jaws, which it then proceeds to crunch; from the gorgeous butterflies of Brazil, larger than a man's hand, to a 'meek-faced' kangaroo disembowelling a dog; from a swarm of hornets stinging to death an incautious sahib, to the fearsome charge of a wounded buffalo.

At times he retails travellers' tales that have provided the basis for a thousand yarns.

Mr Atkinson has sketched, with his usual graphic

vigour, the situation of himself and his party of Kalmucks, when surrounded by wolves in Mongolia. They were encamped for the night on the open steppe on the banks of a little lake, when suddenly the howling of the terrible wolves was heard at a distance. The men quickly collected the horses, and prepared to receive the assailants. The fire was nearly out, but it was thought best to allow them to approach, and then by a little fresh fuel obtain light enough for a fair shot. It was not long before the padding of their many feet was heard as they galloped towards the party, and presently a savage howl arose. The men threw some dry bushes on the embers, and blew up a bright flame, which sent its red glare far around, disclosing the pack with ears and tails erect, and flashing eyes. At a signal, five rifles and a double barrel poured in a volley with deadly effect, as the horrible howling revealed. Snarling and shrieking, the pack drew off, but the Kalmucks declared they would return.

Soon the terror of the horses announced the re-approach of the marauders, and they could be heard stealing round between the encampment and the lake, dividing into two packs, so as to approach on opposite sides. Presently the glare of their eyeballs was seen, and their grizzly forms pushing one another on. Again the bullets sped, and the shrieking packs again retreated, but only to keep watch at a little distance.

One aspect of nature that keenly exercised Gosse, doubtless intrigued by the recent discovery of the gorilla, was the possibility of other unknown species lurking in the unexplored regions of land and sea. As one might expect from the author of *The Ocean*, he speculated particularly about the sea in this respect. 'Who has not felt,' he muses longingly, 'when looking over a boat's side into the clear crystal depth, a desire to go and explore?' How he would have envied the undersea exploits of, say, Jacques Cousteau or Hans Haas!

One of his favourite subjects was the sea-serpent. He discusses at great length the possibility of its existence, citing innumerable claims to support his belief in such a monster. There were the sworn testimonies, a few years back in Norway, of a respectable bookseller, along with a printer and two fishermen, who while boating on Romsdal-fjord claimed to have seen an enormous marine animal between forty and fifty feet in length, with a sharp snout on a colossal head. The bookseller fired at it with his musket, whereupon the sea-serpent dived. But surfacing again immediately with head upraised, it darted after them like some huge snake. The four Norwegians pulled for shore, and the monster only stopped pursuing them when they reached shallow water.

In America, the Linnean Society of New England published a detailed report of a sea-serpent sighted near Cape Ann, Massachusetts, backed up by sworn depositions from eleven witnesses, 'fair and unblemished characters'. Mottled dark brown in colour, the size of a horse, and with a head like that of a rattlesnake, this monster moved like a gigantic caterpillar with vertical undulations. Independently, a respectable colonel testified about the same nightmarish creature: 'As nearly as I could judge, there was visible at a time about forty feet of the sea-serpent's body. The head was flat in the water and the animal was of a chocolate colour. I was struck by an appearance in the front part of the head like a single horn, about nine inches or a foot in length and of the form of a marlinspike.'

In *The Times* of 9 October 1848 came this report:

When the *Daedalus* frigate, Captain M'Quahae, which arrived at Plymouth on the 4th instant, was on her passage home from the East Indies, between the Cape of Good Hope and St Helena, her captain and most of her officers and crew, at four o'clock one afternoon, saw a sea-serpent. The creature was for twenty minutes in sight of the frigate and passed under her quarter. Its head appeared to be four feet out of the water and there was about sixty feet of its body in a straight line on the surface. It is calculated that it propelled itself at the rate of fifteen miles an hour. The diameter of the exposed part of the body was about sixteen inches; and when it extended its jaws, which were full of jagged teeth, they seemed sufficiently capacious to admit of a tall man standing upright between them.

Gosse, convinced that some kind of sea-serpent existed, considered it most likely to have strong affinities with the fossil Enaliosaur, a kind of giant marine lizard. The *Daedalus* controversy raged for a long time, with naturalists of the calibre of Sir Richard Owen weighing

Sir Harry Johnston's portrait (above) is by Keith Shackleton. Johnston himself was an accomplished artist, as his drawing of the okapi (opposite) shows. It was no wonder that the okapi remained so long unknown, for not only does it inhabit some of the most inaccessible country, but it is one of the shyest creatures. Few white men have seen it wild and free even today. Another African animal, that remained even longer unknown to science, was the giant forest hog which Colonel Richard Meinertzhagen discovered in Kenya in 1904.

in adversely and the indignant Captain M'Quahae publishing certified drawings in the *Illustrated London News*.

Gosse's speculations about other unknown animals, as yet unrecognized by zoologists, extended to the land. He pondered, hopefully, that a great anthropoid ape might exist in South America, and cites Humboldt's reports about a 'hairy man of the woods' in the Orinoco region, reputed to build huts, carry off women and devour human flesh. Indians and missionaries firmly believed in this fearsome creature, which they called *Vasitri*, meaning 'The Great Devil'.

Most of all, Gosse believed that there could still be some unknown creature lurking in Africa. He was obsessed with the fact that 'the mighty gorilla himself has only just been introduced to us. What may we not expect of the vast, the uncouth, the terrible, among the teeming wilds of Central Africa?' It could only be in the very centre, for the explorations of Livingstone from the south and Barth from the north had, he laments, even then reduced considerably the extent of unknown land. But in the region lying to the south of Lake Chad and Abyssinia and extending to the equator, it was highly conceivable that much animal life of large dimensions might yet remain hidden. He referred particularly to a fabulous beast resembling the unicorn, rumours of which had been bandied about for the past two or three centuries by Dutch, Portuguese and English traders in West Africa.

As a boy, Sir Harry Johnston came across Gosse's book and, in spite of what he called its maddening piety and evangelical gush, 'rose up from reading it determined some day to explore Africa and to see if I could find any particles of fact to support this story of the unicorn still lingering on in the heart of the continent'. His opportunity came when he was a colonial administrator in Uganda. Meanwhile he chanced upon another clue. In his book *In Darkest Africa* (1890), the explorer H.M. Stanley had mentioned an animal, like a horse or a donkey in appearance, which the pygmies of the Congo sometimes caught in pitfall traps. Stanley said they called it *Atti*, but Johnston later affirmed that the pygmies pronounced the animal's name *O'api*, Stanley having evidently misheard the word.

It was these selfsame pygmies who led Johnston to the 'fabulous' beast whose scientific name commemorates him.

It came about in a bizarre way. Soon after he arrived in Uganda, he had to come to the rescue of a troop of 'Congo Dwarfs' kidnapped by an enterprising German impresario who intended to put them on show in Europe. Because of the Belgian authorities' objections, the German had fled into British territory with his pygmies, who begged Sir Harry to rescue them from his clutches and let them return to their native land.

This was done, and in so doing, and in leading them back to the forests where they dwelt, I obtained much information from them on the subject of the horselike creature which they called the 'okapi'. They described this creature as being like a zebra, but having the upper part of its body a dark brown. The feet, however, had more than one hoof. It was also described as having large, ass-like ears, and a slender muzzle. For a time I thought we were on the track of the three-footed horse, the hipparion, a long-extinct species considered ancestrally related to the horse.

The misunderstanding had arisen because the pygmies insisted that the mysterious creature resembled a horse, which led Johnston to seek the spoor of a single-toed animal. Maddeningly, as he would have said, the pygmies equally insisted that it was cloven-hoofed, like an ox. But while camping in a village he noticed that

. . . the natives used as bandoliers for their guns, or additions to their scanty clothing, handsome marked pieces of hide – brownish black, orange and creamy white. They at once attracted my attention and seemed to me to be the pieces of the skin of an entirely new type of zebra. These, however, I was told, were taken from the okapi whenever it was caught in pit-falls.

So here was Gosse's 'unicorn'; no horse, but a shy relation of the giraffe. One of Gosse's fancies, at any rate, had come true, and the discovery of this unknown animal in 1900 caused a sensation among zoologists. In recognition of his contribution to zoology, Johnston was awarded the Gold Medal of the Zoological Society, an extremely rare honour.

Not everyone was pleased. One professor fired off an angry article to a London magazine declaring that the revelation of the okapi's existence was as nothing in comparison with the discovery of a new death-dealing microbe or a fossil bird.

But if such an 'obvious animal as the okapi, a beast that looked as if it had escaped from a jigsaw puzzle, remained undiscovered up till the beginning of the present century, could not less prominent creatures still exist in those reeking forests in which we seemed in fact to be transported back into Miocene times?' Johnston himself believed so, as did many other people: fifty years ago there was even an expedition to seek out a rumoured Brontosaurus.

A generation before the okapi was discovered, indeed within a few years of Gosse indulging in his speculations, another unknown animal had been brought to light in a far distant part of the world. Gosse himself had suggested China as another possible hiding-place for undiscovered species and it was here that the milu, a hitherto unheard of member of the deer family, was brought to light.

There are no records of the species as a wild animal and it is thought to have become extinct as a feral type through its swampland habitat in Manchuria coming into cultivation or being deforested. A number of animals survived, however, because various emperors of China had kept them in their hunting parks, as in the days of Marco Polo.

In this park, whose wall is sixteen miles in length, the Great Khan keeps game animals of all sorts, such as hart, stag and roebuck, to provide food for his ger-falcons and other falcons which he has in mew. Of gerfalcons alone he possesses two hundred. Every week he comes in person to inspect them in the mews. Often, too, he enters the park with a hunting-leopard on the crupper of his horse; when he feels inclined, he allows it to go free and thus catches a hart or stag or roebuck to give to the gerfalcons in mew. And this he does for recreation and sport.

Needless to say, such hunting-grounds were forbidden territory. Death, and a cruel one, would have been the penalty for any trespasser. But in 1865 the French missionary and naturalist, Père Armand David,

'Recent travellers in Africa,' wrote Philip Gosse, 'have made us somewhat familiar with the mighty and ferocious brutes of that arid continent, the very metropolis of bestial power.' Alas! that metropolis shrinks every year and more and more animals are evicted.

heard rumours of a strange deer that existed in the walled hunting-park of Nan Hai-tzu, to the south of Peking. It was a deer, yet not a deer. It had certain characteristics resembling in turn a stag, a goat, an ass, a cow. And its voice was like that of a donkey braying. Yet still it was a deer!

Père David's curiosity was instantly aroused. He lost no time in visiting the neighbourhood of the imperial hunting-ground. It was useless trying to get permission to enter the park, so he had to content himself with climbing the wall, an exceedingly hazardous thing to do. But to that keen naturalist it was well worth the risk. He sighted the animal in question and there were, he calculated at a rough count, something like 120 in the herd.

Père David was elated. He was confident that he had found a species completely unknown to Western science and he was determined to bring it to the notice of his fellow-naturalists in Europe. For some time he was frustrated in his furtive attempts to obtain tangible evidence that he could send home. But eventually, through means he does not describe, though it could very likely have been by bribing the Tartar guards, he managed to acquire two skins.

> I hastened to have my last shipment for the Museum in Paris properly stowed. It is comprised of the skins of mammals and birds, together with certain botanical specimens. But the most important item of all in this collection is the Sse-pu-hsiang, a kind of large Reindeer of which the female is antlerless. I have attempted for a long time to obtain a specimen of this interesting species of Cervidae, still unknown to naturalists. I know that it exists in considerable numbers in the Imperial Park south of Peking.

Père David's deer was not a reindeer (in any case the reindeer is the sole member of the deer family in which both male and female carry antlers). Its only resemblance to the reindeer was its hoofs. The reindeer has large splayed hoofs to help it travel across snow and, as Richard Lydekker observed in his *Deer of All Lands* (1898), the milu had 'long and widely expanding hooves, which form one of the characteristic features of this species, and are evidently adapted for walking on marshy ground'.

Apart from its slouching shape and its long, tufted

tail, it had another characteristic that distinguished it from its fellow-deer. It differed from all other Old World types in the absence of a brow-tine to the antlers, the posterior prong being as long as the main beam. What was more, as became known eventually, the deer cast its antlers twice a year, unlike the single shedding that took place among other species.

Père David had by his discovery aroused immense interest among Western zoological gardens, between whose directors there was strong competition to be first with the 'new' species. Soon after Père David's original sighting of the herd, the French Legation in Peking contrived to obtain three live deer. They were shipped to France but died on the way. Between 1869 and 1883 the Zoological Society of London acquired four specimens, and a solitary animal ended up in the Berlin Zoo.

None of these efforts would have come to anything

These Père David's deer roam safely in the park at Woburn Abbey, just as their ancestors browsed in the Imperial Park near Peking. Another alien deer that thrived at Woburn was the muntjak or barking deer, having been introduced there about sixty years ago.

but for the interest the Duke of Bedford took in the creature. He became very keen to add Père David's deer to his collection of rare animals at Woburn Abbey. It was fortunate that he did, for in 1895 there occurred one of China's periodical flood catastrophes. The Yunting Ho broke its banks and, among much other damage, destroyed the wall round the imperial hunting-park. The Emperor's collection of animals, including Père David's deer, disappeared, being either swept away by the flood or slaughtered by the stricken populace.

At Woburn, the herd of Père David's deer increased steadily until it numbered several hundred, and several zoos around the world were to benefit from gifts of the animals. The story of the enterprising French priest came full circle in 1960 when the Zoological Society of London was able to send to China a number of deer, descendants of the original strange-looking animals Père David had encountered after boldly scaling the imperial wall.

How delighted Gosse would have been at the discoveries of Père David and Sir Harry Johnston! And to learn of the coelacanth, dredged up from the Indian Ocean in 1938 after being considered extinct for millions of years, not to mention the foul-smelling creature that Japanese fishermen were forced to jettison in 1974 – to the chagrin of scientists. As for the yeti, or 'Abominable Snowman', that has so intrigued our generation, Gosse would surely have mounted an expedition to go in search of it. When, that is to say, he was not sitting in wait alongside Sir Peter Scott on the banks of Loch Ness for the Scottish monster to surface.

19 Many Interpreters

This book would more accurately be sub-titled '*Some Pioneers of Natural History*', presenting as it does no more than a handful of naturalists. To be comprehensive one would need to introduce the many 'literary pioneers' who have brought untold numbers of people to a love and knowledge of nature. Even the rhetoric, some would say the mawkishness, of a Richard Jefferies has instilled in many of us an atavistic longing to regain contact with the natural world. For Man has put aside his contempt for nature; he has, perhaps too late, realized that he is as much a part of the biosphere as the minutest insect.

> It is enough [rhapsodizes Jefferies in *The Story of My Heart*, 1883] to lie on the sward in the shadow of green boughs, to listen to the songs of summer, to drink in the sunlight, the air, the flowers, the sky, the beauty of all. Or upon the hill tops to watch the white clouds rising over the curved hill-lines, their shadows descending the slope. Or on the beach to listen to the sweet sight as the smooth sea runs up and recedes. It is lying beside the immortals, in-drawing the life of the ocean, the earth, and the sun. I want to be always in company with these, with earth, and sun, and sea, and stars by night. The pettiness of house-life – chairs and tables – and the pettiness of observances, the petty necessity of useless labour, useless because productive of nothing, chafe me the year through. I want to be always in company with the sun, and sea, and earth. These, and the stars by night, are my natural companions.

'Intense unnatural feeling' was W.H. Hudson's comment about this kind of writing of Jefferies. Hudson himself was not devoid of feeling, but he kept his emotions on a tighter rein. Not only was he a far more considerable, if untrained, naturalist than Jefferies, but a much more accomplished writer. He was a craftsman, as is a wheelwright or carpenter, working without fuss or embellishment but with strength and effect. Though most of his work was about nature in England, where he settled, perhaps his most influential book was the story of his youth on the pampas of the Argentine, *Far Away and Long Ago* (1918). It is endlessly rich in natural material described in a simple but evocative style. Fraser Darling compared Hudson with a great eagle with the power of seeing intensely.

(Opposite above) Jane Goodall (like George Schaller with the gorilla) could be called a pioneer, for nobody before her had studied the chimpanzee in such detail. Her important, painstaking observations about the social habits of the species, with all their implications for understanding human behaviour and development, were greatly helped by the outstanding photography of Hugo van Lawick – pictured here at work in uncomfortable conditions!
When Jane Goodall first went out to Africa she became an assistant to Dr Louis Leakey, the world-famous palaeontologist and anthropologist who made such important discoveries about prehistoric life in the Olduvai Gorge of Tanzania. It was he who suggested that she should take chimpanzees as the subject for her zoological studies.

(Opposite below) A chimpanzee brandishing a stick – after catching sight of his own reflection in a mirror. But Jane Goodall observed chimpanzees really using 'tools' when they were catching termites. This was one of her most significant discoveries.

One hot day in December I had been standing perfectly still for a few minutes among the dry weeds when a slight rustling sound came from near my feet, and glancing down I saw the head and neck of a large black serpent moving slowly past me. In a moment or two the flat head was lost to sight among the close-growing weeds, but the long body continued moving slowly by – so slowly that it hardly appeared to move, and as the creature must have been not less than six feet long, and probably more, it took a very long time, while I stood thrilled with terror, not daring to make the slightest movement, gazing down upon it. Although so long it was not a thick snake, and as it moved on over the white ground it had the appearance of a coal-black current flowing past me – a current not of water or other liquid but of some such element as quicksilver moving on in a rope-like stream. At last it vanished, and turning I fled from the ground, thinking that never again would I venture into or near that frightfully dangerous spot in spite of its fascination.

But of course he did go back, time after time, in the hope of seeing the black serpent again. One day, disappointed at its failure to appear, he walked on through some nearby mulberry trees where he caught sight of a roosting bat.

Gazing up at this bat suspended under a big green leaf, wrapped in his black and buff-coloured wings as in a mantle, I forgot my disappointment, forgot the serpent, and was so entirely taken up with the bat that I paid no attention to a sensation like a pressure or a dull pain on the instep of my right foot. Then the feeling of pressure increased and was very curious and was as if I had a heavy object like a crowbar lying across my foot, and at length I looked down at my feet, and to my amazement and horror spied the great black snake slowly drawing his long coil across my instep! I dared not move, but gazed down fascinated with the sight of that glistening black cylindrical body drawn so slowly over my foot.

The strangest facet of this enigmatic man was that after he came to England and became an English citizen

This illustration shows two of Jane Goodall's chimpanzees, named Flint and Goblin, interfering when Faber, an adult male, was mating.

Fabre (opposite above) worked in a tiny but teeming world of creatures whose brief lives were full of drama and constant change. Something like 600,000 different kinds of insect have been recorded, and of moths (opposite below) alone there are perhaps 100,000 varieties in the world. Fabre was a lonely man to whom fame was accorded grudgingly. 'For forty years I have struggled with unshakable courage against the sordid miseries of life; and the corner of the earth I have dreamed of has come at last. . . . It is a little late,' he added sadly. A few years before his death, the French Government struck a medal in his honour, showing him characteristically at work with a magnifying glass, peering into the minute kingdom he had made so much his own.

(both his parents were American), he spent most of his time in a boarding-house run by his wife off the Bayswater Road. Yet few men have summoned up so vividly the spirit of nature in general and of the English countryside in particular.

It has been simple enough to present the earliest naturalists, there being only Aristotle and his spiritual descendants groping through the twilight of knowledge and trying to sift fact from fantasy. But of course the ranks of the naturalists have swelled through the ages. Indeed, it is an ironic fact that their numbers have increased in inverse proportion to those of the wild creatures they have studied. But then their work has become more a matter of depth than of breadth. Gone are the days of the 'compleat naturalists' such as John Ray or Linnaeus who could include the entire gamut of nature in their researches. They have been replaced by specialists like Jane Goodall, studying in intimate, brilliant, and even staggering detail, the life of the chimpanzee, and Farley Mowat, holed up for days on end near a family of wolves and displeasing the authorities because he discovered that far from being inveterate killers of big game, the wolves in summer-time on the Barren Lands of Canada fed very largely on mice.

There are some other 'pioneers' who must also be mentioned, however briefly. One is the French entomologist, Jean Henri Fabre (1823–1915), who cut himself off from his contemporaries as surely as did Gosse. But Fabre, even more than the author of *Omphalos*, was perfectly indifferent to this. He had struck up a desultory correspondence with Darwin on the subject of evolution and professed a 'veritable affection' for him, in spite of what he considered to be Darwin's mistaken views. (The French were oddly reluctant to accept Darwin, clinging to their heroes Lamarck and Cuvier long after the rest of the world had honoured the Englishman.)

> I go my own gait [said Fabre], indifferent whether the gallery applauds or hisses. To seek the truth is my only preoccupation. If some are dissatisfied with the result of my observations – if their pet theories are damaged thereby – let them do the work themselves, to see whether the facts tell another story. Patient study alone can throw a little light on the subject.

Patient study was assuredly the keynote of Fabre's work. This is typified by an anecdote he relates about himself in *Souvenirs entomologiques*. One day near his Provençal home, he was sitting by the roadside engrossed in studying a hunting wasp at work. Three peasant women passed by carrying their baskets to the nearby market. On their return in the evening, Fabre was still squatting there, too preoccupied even to greet them. They concluded that he must be mad, crossed themselves as a precaution and hurried on their way out of range of such a sinister figure.

At times when it became too hot, Fabre would try to get his head into a handy rabbit-burrow for a little shade. But when he remembered it he would take an umbrella to protect himself from the southern sun, and this precaution had unexpected results.

> Gadflies of several species used to take refuge under the silken dome of my umbrella, and there they would quietly rest, one here, one there, on the tightly stretched fabric; I rarely lacked their company when the heat was overpowering. To while away the hours

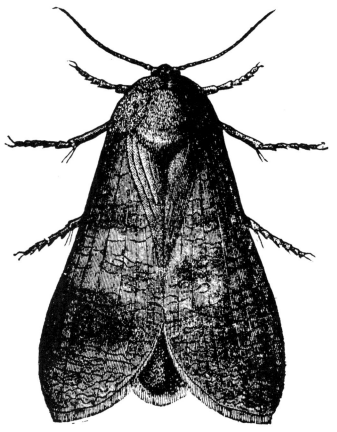

of waiting, I used to love to watch their great golden eyes, which would shine like carbuncles on the vaulted ceiling of my shelter; I used to watch them slowly change their stations, when the excessive heat of some point of the ceiling would force them to move a little.

He was a miniaturist, whose descriptions of the tiny world by which he was fascinated are so exact that it would be an impertinence to condense them. Here he is again watching a hunting wasp, *Philanthus aviporus*, attacking a domestic honey-bee:

Turn by turn, tumbling and tumbled, the two insects roll over and over. But the struggle soon quiets down, and the assassin commences to plunder her prize. I have seen her adopt two methods. In the first, more usual than the other, the bee is lying on the ground, upon its back, and Philanthus, mouth to mouth and abdomen to abdomen, clasps it with her six legs, while she seizes its neck with her mandibles. The abdomen is then curved forward and gropes for a moment for the desired spot in the upper part of the thorax, which it finally reaches. The sting plunges into the victim, remains in the wound for a moment, and all is over. Without loosing the victim, which is still tightly clasped, the murderer restores her abdomen to the normal position and holds it pressed against that of the bee.

The Philanthus has killed the honey-bee in order to feed her larvae; but before carrying it off for the benefit of her offspring

The bandit greedily takes in her mouth the extended and sugared tongue of the dead insect; then once more she presses the neck and thorax, and once more applies the pressure of her abdomen to the honey-sac of the bee. The honey oozes forth and is instantly licked up. Thus the bee is gradually compelled to disgorge the contents of the crop. This atrocious meal lasts often half an hour and longer, until the last trace of honey has disappeared.

But wait! It is not as simple as all that. The patient Fabre, after many hours and days of study, has discovered the real reason for the 'atrocious meal'. The Philanthus does not gorge itself on honey for its own sake. She knows instinctively that while honey to her is ordinary and very acceptable fare, it is, by a peculiar 'inversion', a deadly poison to her larvae!

No wonder Fabre was content to go his own way. He was a scientific Gulliver totally bound up with his insect Lilliputians. One can readily sympathize with the concentrated effort that must have been entailed by his poring over those lowly creatures.

That little miner, the field-cricket, scratches with his fore-claws, but also makes use of the pincers of his mandibles in order to remove pieces of grit or gravel of any size. I see him stamping with his powerful hinder limbs, which are provided with a double row of spines; I see him raking and sweeping backwards the excavated material, and spreading it out in an inclined plane. This is his whole method.

At first the work goes forward merrily. The excavator disappears under the easily excavated soil of his prison after two hours' labour. At intervals he returns to the orifice, always tail first, and always raking and sweeping. If fatigue overcomes him, he rests on the threshold of his burrow, his head projecting outwards, his antennae gently vibrating. Presently he re-enters his tunnel and sets to work again with his pincers and rakes. Presently his periods of repose grow longer and tire my patience.

In all the above there is an echo of Gilbert White, and indeed there is a strong affinity between the Frenchman and Englishman. On the one hand there was the village priest who never stirred from his native land; on the other, the ex-village schoolmaster who wandered no farther afield than his native Provence. Each, like Voltaire's Candide, preferred to cultivate his own garden, aware of the riches of nature on his doorstep. Each wrote with a clarity which brings his subjects into sharp focus as if by the adjusting of a microscope. If White was a portrayer of nature at her most benign, Fabre limned with incisive strokes that other jungle which exists in the insect world.

20 Taking Note

An aspect of the naturalists' work that evokes admiration (especially in relation to the eighteenth and nineteenth centuries) is the devotion given to the writing up of notes and keeping of journals whatever the conditions happened to be. In an age in which even the penning of a letter is avoided when the telephone can be picked up instead, we can only marvel at the sheer physical work involved in those days. Certainly writer's cramp must once have been a common affliction.

For the naturalist, even though he did not write at such length and in such a manner as great novelists like Tolstoy, Dickens and Trollope, the demands were infinitely difficult and strenuous. This was not so for Gilbert White, working in the tranquillity of his study at The Wakes, but for the man in the field it was quite another matter. Whether numbed with cold or aching with hunger, he applied himself with an almost fanatical zeal, knowing only too well that perhaps even more than the colours of the specimens he had collected, human memory fades with every passing moment. Consider Linnaeus squatting in some smoky Lapp tent while he painstakingly recorded his impressions; David Douglas swimming on his back across a flooded river to save his precious writing materials; Darwin, stricken by seasickness, doggedly filling his notebooks; Wallace, shivering with fever in a Sumatran jungle, hastening to gather together his ideas about evolution; Gosse, dripping wet, making his drawings and observations before he would dream of changing his clothes. They lacked even a fountain-pen to make life easier. Not for them a portable typewriter, tape-recorder, camera. And there was no light aircraft, no helicopter, no motor-boat, no overland truck to take them and their gear into the wilds.

Apart from revolutionized communications – transport and radio – two inventions in particular have radically altered the work of the naturalist and the way he is able to present it. The first was the camera – and nowadays more especially the cine-camera. As early as 1881 successful attempts had been made to photograph gannets in the Gulf of St Lawrence. A year later, a Frenchman, Professor E.J. Marey, invented what he called a 'photographic rifle', with which he took shots, as they were appropriately called, of sea-gulls in flight. However, the real pioneers of wildlife photography were the Kearton brothers, Richard and Cherry. Considering

How astonished and delighted Cherry Kearton (pictured here on Richard's shoulders) would have been at the devices used by modern photographers – such as Eric Ashby, who built an artificial badger sett to obtain films of the animal's domestic life.

their heavy plates and cumbersome equipment, which included the now almost forgotten tripod, it is extraordinary how stylish were the results they obtained more than eighty years ago. At times, when confronted by a bird's nest in a tall hedge, Cherry would first have to tie makeshift stilts to the legs of the tripod and then mount on his brother's shoulders to take a picture. Another difficulty was in the recharging of dark slides, which had to be done by means of a changing-bag. One glimpse from Richard Kearton's *With Nature and a Camera* (1897) is enough to illustrate the difficulties entailed. The two men were trying to obtain pictures of a carrion crow's nest and eggs. For this purpose they borrowed a twenty-foot ladder from a farmer, and this had to be placed in a position as nearly perpendicular as possible, otherwise the combined weight of the brothers would have broken the fragile branches of the tree.

When the legs of the tripod had been lashed to the ladder, and the camera focused, my brother's next difficulty was to get his dark slide in and the plate exposed without interfering with the precise adjust-

The use of camouflage for hunting is probably as old as hunting itself. The stalking-horse was a literal fact and horses were specially trained to allow their owners to hide behind them and discharge their 'piece' across their backs. So Cherry Kearton's sheep is in an ancient tradition, even if he was 'hunting' in a somewhat different fashion.

ment of the apparatus. In order to accomplish these feats, he was obliged to hold on to one of the rungs of the ladder with his teeth and thus leave his hands free to work with.

Imagine Cherry Kearton with a telescopic lens! One of the first and best-known attempts at recording bird-song was made in the 1930s. Night after night the 'cellist Beatrice Harrison sat playing in her Surrey garden, hoping that her beguiling music would persuade the local nightingales to join in. Lurking discreetly in the shrubbery, B.B.C. sound engineers waited, equally hopefully, with microphones ready.

While the Keartons were pioneers with the camera, the pioneer of wildlife recording in general was Ludwig Koch, who had been forced to quit Hitler's Germany – one of the many refugees from whom, through the centuries, Britain has reaped benefit. His recordings of bird-song in particular brought pleasure – and instruction – to great numbers of people through radio and 'gramophone' and led to the growth of a nation-wide hobby almost as popular as photography. As for the professional naturalist, the development and refinement of camera and tape-recorder have added new dimensions to his work.

Of course the medium that has truly brought vast audiences, literally hundreds of millions in the Western world, to an awareness of natural history, has been television. In Great Britain, programmes such as the B.B.C.'s *World About Us* or Anglia's *Survival* or films made under the auspices of the National Geographical Association have astonished viewers with detailed glimpses of wild creatures. Whether they are concerned with the huge kingdom of the elephants or the disturbing, almost Martian dance of the insects, television films regularly take us to the threshold of what, to many people, is an entirely new world. For many, this has been a stimulus to go out and see more at first hand, either by bird-watching on the Norfolk Broads, or by joining a safari tour in East Africa, or following the waterway trail in the Everglades of Florida.

As well as evoking a sense of wonder, television ought to alert us to how the marvellous realm of nature is contracting year by year, from the heedless slaughter of otters in Britain to the carnage inflicted upon the rhinoceros

by poachers in Kenya. It is reckoned that since A.D. 1600 around 130 species of wild mammals and birds have been eliminated, through the gun and the trap and especially the destruction of their habitat; and today nearly 250 species are in danger. In the light of such stark facts, it is imperative that we put to positive use our increased knowledge of natural history and our belated awareness of how vitally linked we are with the whole of nature. It would be shameful if the television screen and the zoological garden were the only means by which creatures like the cougar or the orang-utan were to be remembered. Moreover, if Man cannot find room on earth for the rest of nature as well as himself, then before very long he will find himself in a desert place.

Anyone with money can be led to within point-blank range of a big game target by a professional white hunter. It takes infinitely more skill and nerve to shoot with a camera. This picture was taken during the filming of *The Elephant Run* (1977), from the B.B.C. Television series, *The World About Us*.

(Opposite above) Ludwig Koch in the field. His interest in recording started in 1889 when he was a small boy in Frankfurt. 'My father brought home for my brother and me, two Edison photographs and two boxes of wax cylinders. I had the original idea of using my phonograph to record human voices, and just as boys and girls, then and now, would hunt autographs, I surprised well-known people by asking them to give me their autographs by sound on a cylinder.'

(Opposite below) The Spanish imperial eagle taken by one of the most distinguished modern nature photographers, Eric Hosking. This handsome bird, similar in size to the golden eagle, lingers on in the wooded foothills of Spain and is also found in the Balkans and Turkey.

References

Aldington, Richard, *The Strange Life of Charles Waterton.* New York, 1949.

Bates, Henry Walter, *The Naturalist on the River Amazon.* London, 1864.

Blunt, Wilfrid, *The Compleat Naturalist: A Life of Linnaeus.* London, 1970.

Condry, William, *Thoreau.* London, 1954.

Darwin, Charles, *Journal of Researches into the Natural History and Geology of the Countries Visited during the Voyage round the World of H.M.S. Beagle.* London, 1913 ed. (1st ed. 1845).

———, *On the Origin of Species by Means of Natural Selection.* London, 1859.

———, *Autobiography.* London, 1876.

De Beer, Gavin, *Charles Darwin.* London, 1963.

Douglas, David, *Journal Kept by David Douglas during His Travels in North America 1823–1827.* Published under the direction of the Royal Horticultural Society, London, 1914.

Emden, Cecil S., *Gilbert White in His Village.* London, 1914.

Fabre, Jean Henri, *Souvenirs entomologiques.* Paris, 10 vols, 1879–1907.

Garretson, Martin S., *The American Bison.* New York, 1938.

Gosse, Edmund, *Father and Son.* London, 1907.

Gosse, Philip, *The Squire of Walton Hall.* London, 1940.

Gosse, Philip Henry, *A Naturalist's Rambles on the Devonshire Coast.* London, 1853.

———, *Omphalos: An Attempt to Untie the Geological Knot.* London, 1857.

———, *The Romance of Natural History.* London, 1860.

Gourlie, Norah, *The Prince of Botanists: Carl von Linné.* London, 1953.

Hagberg, Knut, *Carl Linnaeus.* Trans. Alan Blair, London, 1952.

Hays, H.R., *Birds, Beasts and Men.* London, 1973.

Herrick, Francis Hobart, *Audubon the Naturalist: A History of His Life and Time.* New York, 1938.

Holt-White, Rashleigh, *Life and Letters of Gilbert White.* London, 1901.

Hooker, William J., *A Brief Memoir of the Life of Mr David Douglas.* London, 1836.

Huxley, Julian, and Kettlewell, H.B.D., *Charles Darwin and His World.* London, 1965.

Jackson, B.D., *Linnaeus* (adapted from the Swedish of Theodor Magnus Fries). London, 1923.

Johnson, Walter (ed.), *The Journals of Gilbert White*. London, 1931.

Johnston, Sir Harry H., *The Story of My Life*. London, 1923.

Kantorowicz, Ernst, *Frederick the Second, 1194–1250*. Trans. E.O. Lorimer, New York, 1957.

Kearton, Richard, *With Nature and a Camera*. London, 1897.

Legros, G.V., *Fabre, Poet of Science*. Trans. Bernard Miall, London, 1913.

Ley, Willy, *Konrad Gesner*. Munich, 1929.

Lockley, R.M., *Gilbert White*. London, 1954.

Matthiessen, Peter, *Wildlife in America*. London, 1960.

Miller, Philip, *The Gardener's and Florist's Dictionary*. London, 1724.

Nash, Roderick, *Wilderness and the American Mind*. New Haven, Conn., 1967.

Pennant, Thomas, *The British Zoology*. London, 1766.

Raven, Canon Charles E., *John Ray, Naturalist: His Life and Works*. Cambridge, 1942.

Roberts, Morley, *W.H. Hudson: A Portrait*. London, 1924.

Schaller, George B., *The Year of the Gorilla*. London, 1965.

Street, Philip, *The London Zoo*. London, 1956.

Thoreau, Henry David, *Walden, or Life in the Woods*. Concord, Calif., 1854.

Turrill, W.B., *Joseph Dalton Hooker, Botanist, Explorer and Administrator*. London, 1963.

Wallace, A.R., *My Life – A Record of Events & Opinions*. London, 1905.

Waterton, Charles, *Wanderings in South America*. London, 1825–52.

——, *Autobiography*. London, 1869.

Wethered, H.N., *The Mind of the Ancient World*. London, 1937.

White, Gilbert, *Natural History and Antiquities of Selborne*. Ed. Thomas Bell, F.R.S., London, 1877.

Whittle, Tyler, *The Plant Hunters*. London, 1970.

Chronology

1650	James Ussher, Archbishop of Armagh, calculates that the Creation took place in 4004 B.C.	1802	Lamarck's *Recherches sur l'organisation des corps vivants.*
1661	John Evelyn publishes *The Smoke of London*, attack on air pollution.	1804	Charles Waterton's South American 'Wanderings' begin.
1662	Grant of royal charter to the Royal Society by Charles II; Robert Hooke invents compound microscope; Wren invents rain-gauge.	1809	Lamarck's *Philosophie zoologique.*
		1812	Cuvier's early work on palaeontology. His 'Catastrophe' theory.
1664	Francesco Redi studies snake venom.	1815	William Smith's geological map published. Battle of Waterloo.
1667	Leeuwenhoek studies human sperm.		
1668	Jan Swammerdam, entomologist, discovers bee-king is really a queen.	1823	David Douglas's first visit to America.
1680	The dodo extinct through excessive hunting by sailors in Indian Ocean.	1827–8	Audubon's *Birds of America* published in Britain.
		1828	Von Humboldt in the Urals; Ernst von Baer tentatively studies mammalian embryology.
1687	Newton publishes *Naturalis principia mathematica.*	1830	Lyell's *Principles of Geology* published.
1693	John Ray attacks Descartes's theory that animals are 'mere machines without feeling'.	1831	Darwin starts his voyage in the *Beagle.*
1730	John Bartram starts first botanical garden in America.	1832	George Catlin on the Missouri and his dream of a national park.
1732	Linnaeus sets out on his Lapland tour.	1839	Joseph Dalton Hooker sets out with Sir James Clark Ross to the Antarctic.
1734	René Antoine de Réaumur starts important work on insects.	1844	Great Auk extinct.
1736	Maupertuis, Buffon's rival, starts polar expedition.	1846	T.H. Huxley voyages in H.M.S. *Rattlesnake.*
1749	Buffon updates Aristotle in *Histoire naturelle.*	1848	Wallace and Bates start their expedition to the Amazon.
1752	Benjamin Franklin invents lightning-conductor.	1853	Gosse's aquarium opens at London Zoo.
1758	Tenth and most important edition of Linnaeus's *Systema naturae.*	1856	Du Chaillu sets out in search of gorilla; Pasteur starts researches into bacteriology.
1768	Sir Joseph Banks sets out with Captain Cook in the *Endeavour.* Lazzaro Spallanzani publishes *Dissertations Relative to the Natural History of Animals.*	1859	The *Origin of Species* published.
		1860	Historic meeting of British Association for the Advancement of Science at which Huxley punctures Bishop Wilberforce.
c. 1768	Petrus Camper tries to inoculate Dutch cattle against foot-and-mouth disease.	1865	Père David discovers hitherto unknown deer in China.
1770	John Hunter, the anatomist, harnesses buffalo to drive through London.	1870–1	Doane-Washburn Expedition to Yellowstone; Franco-Prussian War.
c. 1780	Last wolf in British Isles killed.	1871	Darwin's *Descent of Man* published.
1789	Fall of Bastille, start of French Revolution.	1872–6	Cruise of H.M.S. *Challenger* for study of oceanography.
1797	Solitaire, large flightless bird of Rodriguez Is, Indian Ocean, extinct.	1882	R. Koch makes important advances in microscopy.
1798	Malthus's essay on population.	1900	Discovery of hitherto unknown okapi by Sir Harry Johnston.
1801	Von Humboldt's travels in South America.		

Who's Who

Albertus Magnus (1193–1280). Foremost of several medieval dabblers in natural history such as Thomas of Cantimpré and Vincent of Beauvais. As a cure for excessive drinking he prescribed a mixture of lion's dung and wine. Ended up a saint.

Aristotle (384–322 B.C.). Greek philosopher, tutor to Alexander the Great. First naturalist to systematize his findings. Could be called first evolutionist, propounding a 'ladder of nature' with man at the top.

Artedi, Peter (1709–35). Friend and collaborator of Linnaeus. A zoologist whose fame would have been even greater but for early death. 'Father' of ichthyology, though in this he built on the *Historia piscium* of Ray and Willugby.

Audubon, John James (1785–1851). First artist to go into the wild to study his subjects. 'No man living knows better than I do the habits of our birds; no man has studied them as I have done.' His name is perpetuated not only by his superb paintings but by the National Association of Audubon Societies in North America.

Banks, Sir Joseph (1743–1820). One of the great patrons of natural science but scientist, particularly botanist, in his own right. Best known as companion of Captain James Cook on circumnavigation of the world, but also went on expeditions to Newfoundland and Iceland. President of the Royal Society.

Bates, Henry Walter (1825–92). In 1848, with £100 between them, Bates and Wallace went off to South America and journeyed one thousand miles along the Amazon. Bates subsequently wrote important theses on mimicry among insects, showing how, for example, certain butterflies protect themselves by mimicking unrelated species less susceptible to attack by birds.

Buffon, Count Georges Louis Leclerc de (1707–88). Rich dilettante who inherited 2 million francs when he was seven. As a student he killed a rival swain in a duel and had to flee France. Later settled down and became director of the Jardin du Roi. His catalogue of this turned into his monumental *Histoire naturelle*, much of it a rehash of Aristotle.

Celsius, Olof, sr (*fl.* 1720). Dean of Uppsala who befriended Linnaeus and gave him run of his library. Olof Rudbeck, professor of botany at Uppsala, took Linnaeus into his home but it is said that his wife (like Pharaoh's spouse and Joseph) cast too ardent an eye on the young botanist, who went off to the cooler climes of Lapland.

Culpeper, Nicolas (*fl.* 1640). Popularly far better known than Johnson, but a collector of samples rather than a serious botanist. Summed up by his own dictum, 'He that would know the reason of the operation of the Herbs, must look as high as the Stars.'

Cuvier, Baron Georges (1769–1832). French expert in comparative anatomy. Rejected transmutation of Lamarck; believed, with such as Adam Sedgwick, that catastrophes similar to Noah's Flood had repeatedly destroyed life which was then renewed in fresh round of creation.

Darwin, Charles (1809–82). Darwin was not the 'inventor' of the revolutionary theory for which he is famous. He was a synthesizer of much work that had gone before. In 1813 William C. Wells – an expatriate American – James Pritchard and William Lawrence had put forward hints about natural selection. Edward Blyth, too, between 1835 and 1837, had written articles on the subject in *The Magazine of Natural History*.

Douglas, David (1798–1834). Started botanical career as gardener's boy in Scotland but soon became Collector to the Royal Horticultural Society. Made many botanical and ornithological discoveries during epic journeys in Oregon, British Columbia, California. Died tragically in Hawaii.

Evelyn, John (1620–1706). Silviculturist and diarist, undeservedly neglected. Pepys, his great friend, describes how Evelyn kept a hive of bees in glass 'so you may see the bees making their honey and combs mighty pleasantly'. Evelyn lent house at Deptford to Peter the Great studying shipbuilding and was 'mighty' put out when the Tsar hacked down his fine holly hedge.

Fabre, Henri (1823–1915). Another insect-man. But full recognition was accorded grudgingly to this French schoolmaster. 'For forty years I have struggled with unshakable courage against the sordid miseries of life; and the corner of the earth I have dreamed of has come at last. . . . It is a little late.'

Frederick II, Emperor (1194–1250). Greatest naturalist and most remarkable character of Middle Ages. Contemporary of St Francis of Assissi but was his antithesis except insofar as each in his own way embarrassed the Papacy; St Francis by his emphasis on love and poverty, Frederick by rejecting the authority of the Pope.

Gerard, John (*fl.* 1590). His *Herbal*, published near end of Queen Elizabeth's reign, largely based on Rembert Dodoens's work. He wrote in pleasant if quaint style. Of the milkwort: 'The flower grows at the top of a blew colour, fashioned like a little bird, with wings, tail and body, only to be discovered by those who do observe the same.'

Gesner, Konrad (1516–65). Swiss naturalist handicapped like Turner by his Protestantism, but patrons such as Oswald Mycenius enabled him to study in France. Became the leading zoologist of Renaissance times with his four-volume *Historia animalium*.

Gosse, Philip Henry (1810–88). One of the greatest Victorian naturalists isolated from contemporaries by extreme fundamentalism. But his fine work in marine biology is still valid today. Instrumental in foundation in 1853 of world's first public aquarium at Regent's Park.

Hagenbeck, Carl (1844–1913). Zoos have always been a matter of controversy, but nowadays they undoubtedly have an important role to play in captive breeding and helping to save endangered species. Hagenbeck, although close to the Barnum and Bailey tradition, made many useful innovations in zoo management.

Harvey, William (1578–1677). His work on the circulation of the blood and functioning of the heart opened up a new world in comparative anatomy. According to John Aubrey 'he was wont to say that Man was but a great mischievous Baboon'. A profitable baboon, however, for as a fashionable physician Harvey left £20,000.

Hooke, Robert (1635–1703). British inventor and scientist, Curator of the Royal Society, author of *Micrographia* (1665). According to John Aubrey, Isaac Newton borrowed some of his ideas without acknowledgement. 'I wish Master Hooke had writt plainer and afforded a little more paper.'

Hooker, Sir Joseph Dalton (1817–1911). Like his father, Sir William, eminent botanist and Director of Royal Botanical Gardens at Kew. Naturalist with Sir James Clark Ross's Antarctic Expedition, 1839. His resulting *Flora Antarctica* (1844–7) established his reputation as taxonomist and plant geographer. Great supporter of Darwin.

Hudson, William Henry (1841–1922). Strange, aloof, enigmatic man who, reared among the gauchos of the South American pampas, settled in his wife's boarding-house in London's Bayswater, yet wrote some of the most enduring classics of the English countryside and nature, such as *A Shepherd's Life*, *A Hind in Richmond Park*, *Birds and Man*.

Humboldt, Alexander von (1769–1859). German scientist who attempted to embrace whole realm of nature in his book *Kosmos*, but chiefly famed as world-wide geographer and traveller (his name perpetuated by oceanic current off Peru). Goethe wrote of him 'my natural history studies have been roused from their winter sleep by his presence'.

Hunter, John (1728–93). Regarded as a dullard by his Scottish farming family, put to work in the fields where he acquired a love of nature. Became most famous surgeon of his time and famed for work in anatomy. Given permission to dissect animals in Tower of London Zoo (forerunner of Regent's Park). His fine collection presented to College of Surgeons.

Huxley, Thomas Henry (1825–95). Like Darwin, took part in a voyage of surveying and exploration – in H.M.S. *Rattlesnake* in Australian and New Guinea waters, 1847–50. 'How extremely stupid not to have thought of that,' he exclaimed, on reading The *Origin of Species*. His review of the book in *The Times* was an important factor in its success.

Johnson, Thomas (d. 1644). A considerable botanist cut off in his prime fighting in English Civil War. Published first local list of wild flowers in English; first to study native flora as genuine botanist. Edited Gerard's *Herbal* 1633.

Kepler, Johannes (1571–1630). Czech astronomer who showed that the path of the planets is elliptical. Improved upon system of Copernicus and evolved a 'precise mathematical formula to describe the sun and the planets'. Believed in celestial music.

Lamarck, The Chevalier Jean-Baptiste de (1744–1829). As a boy, a French hero in the Seven Years' War, but remembered chiefly for his *Philosophie zoologique* (1809). First to realize immense age of earth, thinking in terms of millions of years rather than the 6,000 years worked out by Archbishop Ussher and Dr Lightfoot (who even pinpointed the Creation as having taken place at nine o'clock in the morning on 23 October).

Leeuwenhoek, Antony van (1632–1723). Contemporary of Dutch painter Vermeer. Hobby of grinding lenses led to ability to magnify 270 times, vastly better than Galileo's microscope of 1614. Discovered existence of bacteria 1617; function of sperm.

Linnaeus, Carolus (1707–78). 'Prince of Botanists' but chiefly renowned for his binomial system of classification. 'Wisdom's first step' for him consisted of 'affixing a name to each thing to distinguish each from the other' so that knowledge could be communicated among scientists.

Lyell, Sir Charles (1797–1875). Author of *The Principles of Geology* (1830). Henslow advised Darwin to read this but on no account to believe it because of Lyell's caution over possibility of evolution. But Lyell became staunch champion of Darwin.

Newton, Isaac (1642–1727). English scientist renowned for his conception of idea of universal gravitation, but first published work was in optics. Best ideas conceived at home when University of Cambridge closed because of the Great Plague 1665–6. 'In those days I was in the prime of my age for invention.'

Owen, Sir Richard (1804–92). A leading anatomist; Superintendent of Natural History Departments of British Museum 1856–83. Vicious opponent of Darwin and strove to prove there was an unbridgeable gap between Man and the apes. 'Descended from the Apes!' exclaimed the wife of the Bishop of Worcester. 'My dear, let us hope it is not true, but if it is, let us pray that it will not become generally known!'

Phoebus, Gaston (*fl.* 1370–1400). Hunting was for long the chief means of contact with nature. Phoebus and Henri de Ferrières were two late fourteenth-century authors of handbooks on the chase. The Abbess Juliana Berners was patron if not actual author of the *Book of St Albans*, printed in 1486.

Pliny (A.D. 23–79). Roman general turned naturalist. Historian Edward Gibbon described his *Historia naturalis* as 'that immense register where Pliny has deposited the discoveries, the arts and the errors of mankind'. Perished in eruption of Vesuvius that destroyed Pompeii.

Ray, John (1627–1705). English clergyman, universal naturalist whose work on classification greatly benefited Linnaeus. Much helped by patron and collaborator, Francis Willughby. Influenced by Nils Steensen, Danish anatomist and geologist.

Smith, Sir James Edward (1759–1828). Wealthy young English industrialist and amateur naturalist who bought up Linnaeus's great collection for £1,000 and founded the august Linnean Society in 1788 on the basis of it.

Smith, William (1769–1839). Known as 'Father of English Geology' and nicknamed 'Strata Smith'. Worked as surveyor of coal-mines, canals, drainage systems, from which his interest in geology stemmed. A copy of his famous geological map is in the British Museum (Natural History).

Solander, Daniel (d. 1782). Best-known disciple of Linnaeus; accompanied Banks in Cook's *Endeavour*. The family of Sir Joseph's English fiancée accused him of adversely influencing Banks in favour of a Tahitian beauty. Solander also went to Iceland with Banks.

Strabo (d. A.D. 25). Roman geographer whose works were renowned for elegance of style. Travelled widely in search of information and his books were among the two thousand that Pliny drew upon.

Thoreau, Henry David (1817–62). Influential American writer revered by his countrymen. Acquired love of nature as a boy roaming the woods and fields near his birthplace of Concord, Massachusetts. Disciple and helpmate of Ralph Waldo Emerson. Thoreau wrote 'I never found the companion that was so companionable as solitude', an attitude summed up in his classic *Walden, or Life in the Woods*.

Turner, William (*fl.* 1550). Has been dubbed the Father of English Botany and his *Herbal* considered to mark the beginning of science of botany. Dedicated his *Libellus de re herbaria* to Henry VIII; had to flee England under Bloody Mary, but came back and dedicated another book to Elizabeth, reminding her that they had met.

Wallace, Alfred Russel (1823–1913). While Darwin was wrestling with the key to the Origin of Species, he was stunned to find that Wallace had already opened the door – and equally overwhelmed by Wallace's generosity in letting him take all the credit.

Waterton, Charles (1782–1863). Brilliant English field-naturalist to whom, because of his eccentricity, justice has never fully been done. Always insisted on first-hand information. Also greatly in advance of time in realizing need to maintain balance of nature.

White, Gilbert (1720–93). English clergyman who wrote joyously but scientifically about nature. Ahead of his time in realizing territorial significance of bird-song and process of ecology. Chief work consisted of letters to other naturalists, Thomas Pennant and Daines Barrington.

Illustration Credits

Index

Page numbers in *italic* refer to illustrations

Acknowledgements

For permission to quote copyright material, thanks are due
to William Collins Sons & Co. Ltd and the University of
Chicago Press (*The Year of the Gorilla* by George
B. Schaller); A. D. Peters & Co. Ltd and Holt Rinehart &
Winston Inc. (*Bury My Heart at Wounded Knee* by Dee
Brown); Thames and Hudson Ltd (*No Room for Wild
Animals* by Bernhard Grzimek); and Weidenfeld & Nicolson Ltd
(*Primitive Song*, trans. C. M. Bowra).